SAME RED DIRT

A Comical Memoir

Pat Conrad

This book is a narrative nonfiction. The author has tried to recreate events and conversations from his memories of them. Only the names of people have been changed to protect the privacy of individuals and the security of confidential matters.

Same Red Dirt Copyright © 2018 by Lawrence P. Conrad. All Rights Reserved.

No part of this publication may be reproduced, distributed, or transmitted in any form or by any means, including photocopying, recording, or other electronic or mechanical methods, without the prior written permission of the publisher, except in the case of brief quotations embodied in critical articles and reviews, in addition to certain other noncommercial uses permitted by copyright law.

Cover designed by Limelight Book Covers.com
Editing by David Ferris

For additional information or permission requests, email the publisher at
SameRedDirt@gmail.com or visit the author's website at www.SameRedDirt.com

ISBN: 978-0-692-06561-7

Printed in the United States of America
First Edition, 2018

*To my mom, Mona Conrad,
and my "Nannie," Catherine McGinnis,
for being faithful prayer warriors for me
when I was lost and for praying
for the rest of the family.*

*All you "prayer warriors" out there,
pray without ceasing and
never give up on someone...*

ACKNOWLEDGMENTS

THANKS TO MY WIFE, Vicki Conrad, for being my motivator and supporter. She helped to make this book happen by taking dictation as I told my stories and worked diligently in formatting my book for publishing. A special thank you also to my friend Dan Benson, who helped edit the "vomit edition" before turning our manuscript over to a professional editor. David Ferris was our editor and was very helpful and patient in dealing with me as a first-time book writer.

CONTENTS

SAME RED DIRT i
    Acknowledgments v
    Preface xi
    Introduction xv

ROOTS 1
    Daytona Boy 3
    Wood Shop Mischief 5
    From Daytona to Atlanta 9
    The Honeymoon Is Over 11
    What Are the Odds? 15
    A Plan to Leave 21

NEW IN AUSTRALIA 25
    Off to a Great Start! 27
    The Madhouse 31
    The Motorcycle 33

WARD B 35
    Bart a.k.a. "Dummy" 37
    Toilet Seats 41
    The Picnic 43
    Tea Break from Hell 47
    One Good Turn Deserves Another 51
    Cookie Monster 53
    The Night Shift 57
    Fun in the Dungeon 59

WARD C 63
    Grabbing Hold of a Bobcat 65
    The Queen's Birthday 67

WARD D 69
    Broke in Right 71
    Ben 73
    Steve 75
    Jack a.k.a. Hannibal Lecter 77

WARD F 79
    Ooooh That Smell 81
    Peas, Carrots, and Corn 83
    Charlie 85
    Uh-Oh 89

LAST MONTH AT THE MADHOUSE 91
    Like a Paid Vacation 93
    Draft Dodging 97
    Preparing to Hit the Road 99

LIVING ON THE EDGE 101
    Dirt Road to HELL! 103
    Moving On… 109
    Who's There? 111

THREE WEEKS AT THE MELBOURNE HOSTEL 113
    Extended Stay 115
    Week One 117
    Week Two 119
    Week Three 121

TASMANIA 125
Beggars Can't Be Choosy 127
A Night to Remember 131
Where There's a Will, There's a Way 137
The Scientific Method 139
Making Plans 141

BACK TO THE MAINLAND 143
Kick-A-Rock Trick 145
It's Worse Than We Thought! 147
Tripping Grass 149

TWENTY-TWO DAYS AT SEA 151
Leaving a Dream Behind 153
Rude and Crude 155
Night Moves… 157
New Zealand and the Fiji Islands 159
Acapulco 161
How *Not* to Stop a Ship 163
Tension in Panama 165
Time for Soul-Searching 167

BACK IN AMERICA 169
Going Through Customs 171
Seek and Find 173
Cheap Shots 177
Moment of Truth 179
Keeping It Real 181
Epilogue 183
About the Author 185

PREFACE

THIS BOOK IS WRITTEN about events in my life that happened around half a century ago. The names of the people in this book have all been changed to protect the innocent, as well as the "guilty." Everything I'm about to tell you is true, to the best of my memory. My stories will take you on my wild and crazy journey when I traveled ten thousand miles from home to Australia. Most of the events took place during a 13-month period, from April 1971 to May 1972. I don't know if these events are "normal" or not; I'll let you be the judge of that. Little did I know that this time would impact me for the rest of my life.

"You will seek me and find me when you search for me with all your heart."

--Jeremiah 29:13 NIV

SAME RED DIRT

A Comical Memoir

Pat Conrad

INTRODUCTION

WHEN AS A YOUNG MAN, Pat Conrad gave up a good job and left the United States in search of greener pastures in Australia, he didn't know what he would find—or even if he would come back at all. During the next thirteen months, his freewheeling spirit and thirst for adventure brought him in contact with a parade of unforgettable characters. With refreshing honesty and a keen wit, *Same Red Dirt* recounts Pat's experiences working at Sydney's infamous Callan Park Mental Hospital, where he spent time among some of the world's most criminally insane; his escape to the sandy beaches near Sydney; his hair-raising experiences down the red dirt roads of Australia's rugged Outback; and his series of unusual jobs as he made his way throughout the country. In this "R-rated Christian memoir," Pat shares how his bad choices along the way, and his desire to fill a hole in his heart, led to a major change in his life.

ROOTS

Daytona Boy

I WAS BORN AND RAISED in Daytona Beach, Florida, where my mother managed hotels. She worked hard as a single mom to support and raise my older brother Mike and me. We were close as a family, and I had some good friends growing up as well.

For example, Luke was a friend of mine from junior high school and probably the wildest person I have ever known. I once made the mistake of getting on the back of his motorcycle. He drove like a madman, speeding recklessly between cars like a demon from hell. I didn't think I would come out of it alive! Luke was legally driving a motorcycle in junior high because he was older than I was, I guess because he had failed a grade or two. I suppose, my association with Luke conveyed that I started out young, occasionally hanging out with a bit of wild and crazy…

Wood Shop Mischief

AT SEABREEZE JUNIOR HIGH School in Daytona Beach, I had a teacher named Mr. Walters. He was a tall, lanky, balding man in his forties. He taught my wood shop class, an all-male class of rowdy boys, and at that age, the testosterone levels were high. When there was bad behavior, Mr. Walters gave you two choices: either write, "I will behave in wood shop class" five hundred times; or three licks with a paddle at the start of the next day's class. Being the macho young men that we considered ourselves to be, we always went with the three licks.

Mr. Walters' paddle was actually two long paddles glued together at the handle, leaving a gap between the "business" part of the paddle. When you got spanked with it, the paddle made a loud smacking sound twice, so we nicknamed it the "Double Whammy." The start of each day's class was always interesting because there was always someone who was going to get a paddling. One classmate thought he would be clever and before class, folded up a pillowcase and put in his pants. When Mr. Walters hit him with the first lick, it made a *psssst* sound, like letting the air out of a balloon, and the entire class, including Mr. Walters, burst out laughing. The student was told to remove the pillowcase, and then Mr. Walters gave him his three licks.

Sometimes when Mr. Walters left the class, we would sneak out his paddle, look for an unsuspecting student busy standing, working on his wood-making project, and give him a surprise lick as a joke. Obviously, this would cause quite a commotion and a chain reaction of unruly behavior on our part. Thankfully, the wood shop building was a distance from the rest of the classrooms since we could get pretty loud at times.

One day when Mr. Walters left the room, my crazy friend Luke and I decided to trade licks with each other as hard as we could. A crowd of guys gathered around. Luke leaned over a table and I reared back with the paddle and hit him as hard as I could square on the butt. He jumped around holding his backside and turned red in the face.

Then, a wild-eyed look came over Luke, and I knew I was in trouble. I hadn't considered that he would have the opportunity to retaliate. Luke was taller and bigger than I was, but there was no backing out now since we had a crowd watching.

Dreading what was coming, I leaned over the table and braced myself for Luke's payback swing. As I was leaning over the table, I turned my head around only to see Luke airborne, with both feet off the ground. He swung the paddle so wildly that instead of striking me with the flat side of the paddle, he hit my butt with its side edges. It wasn't macho for guys to holler, but like Luke, I jumped around holding onto the seat of my pants. Later, when I went to the bathroom to check the damage done, I saw two dark red stripes across my butt cheeks.

Mr. Walters never missed a day, but one day later that school year, we filed in the wood shop classroom and were surprised to see an unfamiliar man standing in front of the room. He was middle-aged with a flat-top haircut, was about five foot ten and of stocky build, and he wore dark sunglasses indoors.

We ignored the guy and carried on our usual loud conversations and undisciplined, disruptive behavior. But when the bell rang,—our signal to begin class,—our substitute teacher started shouting, "Didn't you hear that bell go off? That means you SHUT UP and you listen to what *I* say!"

Obviously, he got our attention. As we quieted down, he continued yelling, "I heard this was an unruly class! Well, not anymore! See these sunglasses? When you think I'm looking over here, I'm NOT! I'm looking at YOU! The military taught me how to kill a man nine different ways, so I am NOT intimidated by YOU PUNKS!" Then, a bit calmer, he said sternly, "You will be having a quiz tomorrow, so you had better pay attention!"

"He may not be intimidated, but we sure were!" I thought to myself. Amazingly, we managed to get through the rest of the class with no incidents.

Later, some of us guys got together to talk between classes. Luke said, "Wow, what's with this guy? He must have been a drill instructor!" Even though we were a bit frightened by this substitute teacher, we thirteen- and fourteen-year-old boys conspired to jerk his chain.

The next afternoon, as we filed into class prepared to take our "quiz," I laughed to myself about what was about to take place. As soon as the bell rang, our substitute teacher began walking around the classroom, handing out the quiz he had promised. As each of us "conspirators" received our test, one at a time, we took out a pair of dark sunglasses and put them on. We figured if we couldn't see his eyes, then he wouldn't be able to see ours if we cheated during the quiz. After he passed out all the tests and walked back to sit down at his desk, he looked out at the class to discover what we had done. He may have been human after all, because I thought I saw a hint of a smile. But it quickly disappeared, and he said in his stern voice, "Take your sunglasses off. Boy, you guys really *are* smart-asses!"

And boy, was he right!

From Daytona to Atlanta

LUKE AND I WERE GOOD BUDDIES, but I lost contact with him after junior high school. I wondered if he had moved away or dropped out, as I never heard from him again.

I possess an intense love for the beach—saltwater flows through my veins. My brother Mike and I worked during the summer as lifeguards at various beach hotel pools. Basically, as a teenager, any time that I wasn't in school, sleeping, or working out with weights, I was on the beach. Concentrating at Seabreeze High School was often a challenge when I could look out the window with envy and see people walking up and down the beach.

* * *

Besides the beach, my other passion was lifting weights. From ninth to twelfth grade, I had doubled my body weight thanks to bodybuilding. During my senior year, I even entered a Teenage Mr. Florida competition. There were 12 guys in the competition and I came in fourth. Not too bad for my one and only bodybuilding competition.

My brother was also a bodybuilder, and he and I spent a lot of time pumping iron in our garage, across the road and two houses over from Greg and Duane Allman, who would later become the world-famous Allman Brothers Band. We got to work out listening to the pounding drums and electric guitar riffs of the Allman Brothers!

After my high school graduation, Mama moved to Atlanta to take a job. She worked downtown at the Hyatt Regency Hotel, managing the cashiers and the cash flow. Temporarily, Mike and I stayed in Daytona with our grandmother, Nannie, to lifeguard. That fall I attended one semester at Daytona Beach Junior College and by the next summer, the summer of 1968, Mike and I had moved to downtown Atlanta with Mama. We got jobs lifeguarding at the Marriott Hotel. Mama worked nearby at the Hyatt, which was one of the most upscale hotels in Atlanta and enabled my mom to meet a lot of influential people. One of these people held an international management position at Delta Airlines and was kind enough to give me a recommendation for a job.

After a short training class, at age 19, I was happy to land my first full-time job with good pay and good benefits, including awesome discounts on flights—a perk that would serve me well later. I was hired as a baggage handler and settled in quickly and was enjoying the extra money in my pocket.

One afternoon, during my first year at the Atlanta airport, I went upstairs to the public concourse to book a flight to Las Vegas for a vacation. As I was crossing the busy concourse, suddenly, someone said, "Hi, Pat!" I looked around and with great surprise saw that it was Luke, my long-lost friend from junior high, sporting a GI haircut and dressed in an Army uniform. He told me he was passing through Atlanta on his way to Vietnam. We hurriedly talked for just a few minutes, as I had to get back to work and he had to catch a flight. "*What are the odds*," I thought, knowing that thousands of people pass through that terminal every day, that I would run into him on one of only two times that I ever went upstairs to the public concourse? But knowing Luke was going to Vietnam, I didn't know if I would ever see him again.

The Honeymoon Is Over

AFTER THREE LONG YEARS working for Delta, my honeymoon with the airlines was over. I never had a holiday off and had to work weekends. I worked outside either in the heat or the cold, and my crazy work schedule was killing me. Every week I had to rotate shifts in a schedule so brutal and irregular that sometimes, literally, I didn't know if I was coming or going. As soon as my body adjusted to one shift, the shift changed, and I had to adjust all over again.

My schedule had me rotating shifts from 7:00 in the morning to 3:30 in the afternoon; from 3:30 p.m. until 11:00 p.m.; and from 11:00 p.m. until 7:00 a.m. This regimen had me so confused that one time I almost went to work twice on the same day! After working the 7:00 a.m. to 3:30 p.m. shift, I came home and took a nap until 6:00 p.m. When my alarm went off, I thought it was 6:00 in the morning, so I rushed to put on my uniform pants and shirt only to realize that I'd already been to work that day.

The exhausting summertime heat toiling in the bin (or belly) of the planes and the painfully cold winters, when the wind whipped us almost constantly, took their toll on me. But in spite of stress and discomfort, it was still a good job because they paid us well. Every time the unionized airlines gave employees a raise, Delta, although it was not unionized, would match it as a tactic to keep the union out. My first year I received an across-the-board pay raise that everyone got along with two merit pay raises, in addition to a Christmas bonus. My job with Delta enabled me to trade in my not-so-cool, not-so-powerful six-cylinder Mustang for a cool V-8, 351 Mach1 Mustang, baby blue with sleek red pin stripes. Today, that classic car would be worth a lot of money!

Delta had high standards for their employees, requiring a clean cut, all-American look. However, unlike Delta, Eastern Airlines was unionized, so their employees were allowed to have long hair and beards. Most of my high school friends were hippies now and had long hair, as it was the late 60s and the hippie movement was in full swing. The rebel in me made me envy the employees' freedom at Eastern. Ironically, today, almost fifty years later, Delta is still in business and Eastern closed their doors in 1991.

One night on the graveyard shift, at 2:00 a.m., a supervisor walked up to me and said, "Pat, you have a five o'clock shadow. You need to shave."

"Yes, sir," I answered. But I was thinking that at two o'clock in the morning, none of the customers would even notice. The customers just wanted their baggage to arrive safely at its destination at the same time the customers did; they couldn't care less about an airline employee's facial hair.

Being upset about Delta's petty appearance code further inflamed the rebellious nature that was pumping through my veins at that time in my life. Frustrated by these minor injustices and having grown tired of working outdoors in the cold, I considered the possibility of transferring to a warmer climate. Recently Delta had enlarged Ft. Lauderdale Airport, on South Florida's east coast. They were interviewing employees who wanted to transfer. Before I knew it, I found myself en route on a flight to Ft. Lauderdale.

Working in South Florida was a relief compared to working in the bitter cold winters of northern Georgia. However, being at a much smaller airport with fewer employees meant that we had to juggle multiple responsibilities. "The bag handlers," some of the employees would say, "have to do everything but fly the airplane." It was a very physically demanding job. In addition to loading and unloading baggage, and dealing with the stress of ensuring everyone's luggage got to the right destination, we had to fill the plane's water tank from the water truck. We also had to go on board to clean the plane, haul away all the garbage, and perform everybody's favorite job, "dump the crapper." Evidently my new job wasn't as great as I had thought. Sometimes in life we must learn the hard way that the grass is *not* always greener on the other side.

On the graveyard shift, working 11:00 p.m. to 7:00 a.m., we would try to make the best of hauling off the garbage to the dumpster. To have the planes clean and ready for their next flight, we were responsible for throwing out the leftover food from the first-class section. Sometimes the meals consisted of filet mignon steaks. We thought, "Why waste perfectly good steaks?"

The dumpster was a long distance from the terminal and, consequently, poorly lit at night. Sitting on our tugger in the dim light, we would gorge ourselves with delicious, mouth-watering steaks, and wash them down with vodka from the small bottles that they served on the plane. We knew no one would miss the steaks since they would be thrown in the trash, but taking unopened bottles of vodka would have, no doubt, gotten us fired on the spot. Compared to other liquors, I figured vodka was not as noticeable on my breath. The stewardesses were most likely required to keep a running count of the bottles, but we were fortunate that our misbehavior never caught up with us.

What Are the Odds?

ONE DAY WHEN I WAS DRIVING a baggage tugger toward our headquarters, I spotted a man leaning over the short chain link fence that surrounded the airport. I knew he didn't work for Delta since he wasn't in uniform. As I got closer, I saw the man was leaning over the airmail carts, pawing through the canvas bags full of letters and packages and parcels. The guy picked up one bag and threw it roughly to the side, then continued searching through other bags.

As I approached, the man seemed to get more and more nervous, looking up toward me and back behind him. Then, all of a sudden, just like in a movie, a car sped up to him and screeched to a halt as the driver threw open the passenger door! The mail thief dove into the car, slamming the door, and they sped off in a cloud of dust.

I reported this incident to my supervisor back at headquarters. My supervisor didn't get too excited about it, but he did mention that stealing mail was a federal offense. That was the last I heard of it. Little did I know that this incident would later come back to haunt me.

Time passed, enduring my mundane routine of going to work day after day. One of these days, on the way to work on a busy Friday, driving in bumper to bumper traffic, a car beside me started honking its horn loudly. I looked over at the driver who was waving at me frantically. Luke! Evidently, he had managed to survive Vietnam! I almost didn't recognize him because he had swapped his clean-cut GI look for shoulder-length hair, a mustache, and beard. I pulled off to the side of the road, and Luke did the same so we could swap phone numbers. We agreed to get together that night. What were the odds that we would randomly run into each other again, over 600 miles from Atlanta in heavy traffic?

That evening, Luke came over to my apartment to catch up on old times and we smoked a couple Acapulco Gold marijuana joints with the intention of going out to a bar later. We put on a record, and the living room filled with pungent marijuana smoke as we sat there laughing and reminiscing and trading stories. Suddenly, there was a heavy knock at the door, sounding sharply through the music. As I opened the door, before me stood two serious-looking men in business suits. They held up their FBI badges and asked, "Mr. Conrad, can we come in and talk with you?"

Shocked, and almost speechless, like a dumbass, I replied, "Yes." I looked across the hazy room at Luke, sitting on my couch with his eyes as large as silver dollars. I was wondering what Luke had done to bring the FBI down on us and I'm sure he was wondering the same about me.

Baffled about why the FBI would want to speak to me, one of the guys said, "Mr. Conrad, we understand you witnessed the attempted theft of mail at the airport about three months ago." *What are the odds* that they would show up at my door at this awkward time!?!

"We'd like you to take a look at some mug shots," the agent said. Needless to say, I breathed a deep sigh of relief that we weren't the targets of a federal drug bust.

The entire time the FBI agents were in my apartment, I nervously wondered how they didn't notice that the room reeked of marijuana and was filled with smoke. Two marijuana stubs, which pot smokers call "roaches," were lying conspicuously in an ashtray on my coffee table. I cringed as one the agents proceeded to push the incriminating ashtray aside to spread out the mug shots for me to preview. The agent showed me over half a dozen mug shots, and despite my anxiety, I examined the photos carefully until I was able to pick out the man who had been trying to steal a bag of mail. But the guy in the photo had dark hair and the man at the airport was blonde. The agent responded that they had heard his hair had been bleached blonde. He thanked me for my cooperation and both agents left.

As the door closed behind them, I couldn't help but think then—and still think to this day—that the two FBI agents must have laughed all the way back to the office after they first opened my door and saw the expression on my and Luke's face. But then again, I may have had the last laugh as they probably couldn't even pass a drug test after inhaling all the smoke in my apartment. The FBI agents never said anything about the marijuana to me or Luke, but I highly suspected that they must have reported it to my boss at Delta. Not too long after this incident, anti-drug posters were posted on the walls in the employee break room.

Shortly after the FBI left, Luke and I went to meet Ricardo, a friend of Luke's. Ricardo was a sharp dresser and was driving a hot exotic sports car. From his expensive taste in clothes and wheels, I strongly suspected he was a drug dealer. We left Luke's car in a parking lot and rode with Ricardo in his sports car, heading for a popular hippie Ft. Lauderdale nightclub called The Parrot. On the way there, Ricardo lifted up part of the carpet between the bucket seats, unlocked a secret compartment, and pulled out a joint that looked like a cigar. We passed it around, all three of us smoking it on the way to the nightclub. It was so powerful, that we had to put it out before it was even half smoked. I believe it might have been laced with angel dust. Whatever it was, I know that it was a drug much stronger than marijuana.

We arrived and took our place in the long line to get into The Parrot. Finally, we made it to the front. The bouncer at the door was talking with a lady in her thirties as I was showing him my ID. The lady smarted off as she looked me up and down and said to the bouncer, "My, my, my! Letting young boys in this place now?"

I'm usually not that quick on my feet and tend to be shy, but I suppose the drugs smoked earlier were giving me a confidence boost, because I immediately snapped back, "…and old ladies, too?"

The bouncer burst out laughing, patted me on the shoulder, and said, "For that, you get to go in free!"

No sooner had we walked into the nightclub when two beautiful girls approached and grabbed Ricardo, one on each arm, and walked away with him. No doubt, Ricardo was in a whole different league than us. We didn't see him again until closing time when he came to drive us back to Luke's car so we could go home.

The Parrot was known for their "seven for five" deal: seven eight-ounce draft beers in glasses for five dollars, and all seven beers came at one time. I'm not much of a drinker, but that night I downed 21 beers and Luke had 28. Between the two Acapulco gold joints that we smoked before we left my apartment, Ricardo's special cigar on the way, and now the multiple beers, Luke and I were quite wasted. My ears were ringing and all the noise in the bar sounded like a chicken house. Nothing was understandable. Two nice-looking girls came by and sat at our table to try to carry on a conversation with us, but when one of the girls would speak to either me or Luke, we would just look at each other and burst out laughing, too wasted to understand a word they were saying. The girls finally got frustrated with us and got up and left. Luke and I exchanged glances and burst out laughing again.

Not long after, Luke and I saw two undercover policemen going from table to table checking IDs to see if people in the club were of legal age. Luke and I were, but we were paranoid that they would know we were high out of our minds. As the police officers got closer to our table and our paranoia worsened, I was somehow able to utter, "Luke, just be cool. Be cool."

He didn't respond. "Luke, did you understand me?" I said, but as I turned toward him in my wasted state, I poured my drink all down my chest, causing another outburst of laughter from both of us. The two officers walked by and never checked our IDs.

I don't remember much more about that night; in fact, I don't even remember how I got home to my apartment. All I know is, at some point I must have gotten up out of my bed to use the bathroom and I passed out face down between the bedroom carpet and the vinyl flooring in the bathroom. When I woke up in that same position the next morning, I raised my head up off the floor only to see the two different color floors under my eyes and was so disoriented that I had no idea where I was. Trying to sort out the confusion of the two different floors in my mind, I raised myself up and flipped over, only to knock the bathroom door back hard again the wall. The door bounced back, hitting me hard in the back of the head. A great start to a new day!

This happened to be one of my rare weekends off—fortunate, considering how desperately I needed time to recuperate from my crippling hangover. Being high for an entire day and a half, with colors flashing across my eyes like red, yellow, and blue meteorites, was a bit scary to say the least. I was getting a little worried about being high for so long, but the side effects finally wore off and I was back to work on Monday. That was *definitely* a weekend that I would like to forget!

A Plan to Leave

THINGS WERE FINE AT WORK, but Luke was beginning to become a nuisance at my job. At random times, he would park his dull turquoise Volkswagen hippie van at the entrance of the Delta ticket terminal and come in to have a ticket agent page me. He usually left the motor running, loud rock and roll music blaring, and a thin cloud of marijuana smoke emanating out of the windows, --a scene that would have put Cheech and Chong to shame.

While Luke, with his long shoulder-length hair, mustache, and beard, was shameless about his countercultural identity, I was still trying to be a closet hippie. Luke's grand entrances worried me that I would look guilty by association in the eyes of my conservative supervisors. By that time, I was privately scheming up plans to leave my job, but I sure didn't want to get fired prematurely because of bad choices by Luke.

* * *

My frustration with my job was building and the tension in America during that time escalated the feelings that were eventually to change my future. The increasingly chaotic Vietnam War was sowing division in a country marked by frequent demonstrations, protest marches, and flag burning. In the spring of 1968, Martin Luther King, Jr. was murdered, and in the aftermath of the assassination of the leader of the Civil Right Movement, blacks started rioting throughout the country.

Visiting Australia had been a dream of mine for some time. I had always wanted to travel to another country and I preferred one where the people spoke English. Australia is approximately the same size as the

United States, but is a lot less populated. I figured fewer people, fewer problems. Also, it appealed to me that they had a lot of beaches and Australians, as a rule, seemed to have a love for the outdoors like I do.

With all the turmoil in America, I came up with a plan to escape to Australia. I had built up 18 days of vacation time with Delta, and as an airline employee, I could fly free from Florida to California. Knowing that the airlines work together, I contacted Pan American World Airways and found out that they were willing to let me fly free from California to Hawaii and from there on to Sydney, Australia. I had anticipated a discount, perhaps, but had not expected to get to fly all the way at no cost. I was elated at this unexpected turn of events since my finances were limited.

Pan Am actually gave me the tickets that I would need to fly to Australia, but my boss for Delta had to sign off to validate them. When I submitted them for his approval, he refused to sign off because he said the free tickets should be reserved for management and not for baggage handlers like me. I hadn't had many prior dealings with this boss, but realizing what a jerk he could be only confirmed my decision to carry out my escape plan. I was undeterred by this setback; I had decided to go, and nothing would sway me from the course. I still managed to get an 80 percent discount on my tickets with Pan Am and my 18-day vacation was approved. Little did my supervisors know, I had another, much grander plan in the works.

Unaware of the major impact the upcoming months and year would have on the rest of my life, I proceeded with my plan and got my passport to leave the country. In confidence, I shared my plans with my co-workers and several of the guys said they wanted to go with me, but one by one, they backed out. I thought about asking Luke, but I knew that since he wasn't an airline employee, there was no way he could afford the tickets all the way to Australia. But then again, I thought, even if he could afford to go, he was a bit too wild to hang out with all the time. So now I was on my own, on the verge of traveling almost 10,000 miles to a foreign country, fully aware that

I wouldn't know a soul when I got there. Following through took a lot of guts, or perhaps I was just crazy. I guess you can be the judge of that.

The big day finally arrived. I packed my Mustang and headed north, home to Daytona Beach. From there, my brother Mike drove me to Orlando International Airport to catch my four-and-a-half-hour flight to Los Angeles. The ride there was pretty quiet as Mike knew my mind was set on leaving. Since my mom was in Atlanta, there were no emotional goodbyes.

On my short layover in L.A., I proceeded with the next step in my plan. In my craftiness, I had already prepared a hand-written note along with a stamped envelope ready to be mailed. I found an airport mailbox and dropped in my notice to my boss. It read, *Dear Sir: Please count my current approved 18-day vacation as my official two-week notice as I do not plan to return.* Also, I asked him to mail my final paycheck to my mom's address in Atlanta. Knowing that I was giving up a good job, I was relieved to have this part of my plan over with.

Excited to be leaving the mainland of my country for the first time, I transferred to a Pan Am plane and made my five-hour flight from California to Hawaii. There I switched to a 747 and flew a long ten and a half-hour non-stop flight to my destination: Sydney, Australia. That's a long time to fly over that much water! I must admit, I had a few butterflies in my stomach as I thought nervously about what might lie ahead. But I also thought, "No turning back now."

NEW IN
AUSTRALIA

Off to a Great Start!

I AM ONE OF THOSE PEOPLE who can't sleep when traveling, whether in a car or plane. With twenty hours of travel time and going through all those time zones, by the time I got to Sydney, I was like a walking zombie.

For this trip, I had taken a large foot locker with all my possessions, not knowing when or even if I would return. I also carried with me a green leather pouch that had my passport in it, along with $800 in traveler's checks.

When I arrived at the Sydney airport, I promptly cashed a one-hundred-dollar traveler's check into Australia's currency for cab fare and to pay for a motel room for the night. Next, I caught a cab, helping the driver load the bulky foot locker into the trunk.

"Can you recommend a good place for me to stay for the night?" I asked.

"Kings Cross is where a lot of the nightlife is," he replied. "I know a good hotel in downtown Sydney."

I agreed, and we headed to the hotel. When we arrived, I got out of the cab and helped the cab driver take my heavy footlocker out of the trunk. I paid him with cash, and after the driver drove off, I got a bellman at the hotel to help me with my foot locker.

Then it hit me. "Oh, my God!" I realized that I had set my green pouch on the roof of the cab when I got out and totally forgot about it! The cab driver had driven off with my passport and $700 worth of traveler's checks sitting on the roof of his cab in downtown Sydney! I was devastated: one hour in Sydney and already I'd lost my means to legally and financially survive!

But first, I had other matters to attend to. Not sleeping in over twenty-four hours, traversing multiple time zones across the massive Pacific in a cramped plane had left me in a semi-delirious, zombie-like state. I managed to pay for a hotel room for the night and slept for over twelve hours straight. When I woke up, revived, but still suffering from jet lag, I immediately set about resolving my problem of having no passport or money. I was almost 10,000 miles across the ocean, away from home, family, and friends, and in serious trouble.

I recalled from movies that if you are an American and in trouble abroad, you should go to the American Embassy. I checked at the front desk at the hotel, and as luck would have it, the embassy was only two blocks away. Eagerly, I walked the short distance, hoping all the way there to find help or some solution to my dire predicament.

When I arrived, I explained my situation to the receptionist. Her eyes lit up at the words "green leather pouch" and she said, "Hold on a moment!" The lady hurried back into another room and, amazingly, returned with my leather pouch! Man, I was relieved! She explained that a man had turned it in to her the day before and said he had found it on a street curb a few blocks away. As you can imagine, it was a major weight off my chest to have my passport back along with all my traveler's checks!

The receptionist told me the man left his name and address, so when I left the embassy, I converted all my traveler's checks to Australian dollars and mailed the man a monetary reward, along with a thank you note for being honest. At the time, I had no idea about the currency exchange rate, and I later learned that I had mailed him the equivalent of a week's wages for a blue-collar worker.

* * *

The Kings Cross was a strip, like the strips most tourist cities have, where the night life was happening—with busy restaurants, brightly lit gift shops, and rowdy night clubs. The air smelled of fish and chips, meat pies, and booze. I had money in my pocket and was eager to explore.

As I was walking around the strip, two pretty girls approached me and asked me if I was an American. Then they asked if I was a GI and I answered, "No." They explained to me that a lot of GIs came to Australia from Vietnam on R & R (Rest and Recreation), and they thought I was in the military because of my short hair and clean-cut look. It turned out these two girls worked for an Israeli named Levi who had a big rental house with a lot of bedrooms. Levi had a small Afro and fidgety hands that he couldn't keep still. He was a go-getter and was determined to make money any way he could. He operated the rental house by day and worked as a male go-go dancer at night. He had a pretty girlfriend, but his slightly feminine mannerisms made me think he was probably bisexual. As it turned out, Levi had five to six girls who were working the strip to recruit GIs to stay at his house. Their spill was, you can come stay at his house for less money, eat three good meals, meet girls, and have access to drugs versus staying in a boring hotel room.

Since I didn't know a soul in the whole country and the fact that staying at Levi's house was less money and involved girls and drugs, I decided to go with the flow. The girls with their smooth sales pitch managed to recruit not only me, but several GIs.

I crossed the threshold of the house and into a marijuana smoke-filled room full of people getting wasted and listening to the blaring music of Jimi Hendrix's "Purple Haze." It didn't take me long to blend right in and I thought how cool it was that I was now in Australia only two days, and after only the second night I was smoking dope beside a good-looking girl who was half-white, half-Aborigine.

Having the meals provided at Levi's seemed convenient at first, but I soon learned that the meals weren't all that. Cereal and milk were available for breakfast and frequently it was just spaghetti for supper. We couldn't take advantage of lunch since we were usually out of the house in the middle of the day.

After only a few days, some of my personal belongings (first a hairbrush, then a pair of scissors) started disappearing. I figured one or more of the girls must have been ripping me off. With so much traffic coming in and out of the house, it was only a matter of time before something major was stolen from me. So, I decided I'd rather have my own place to stay.

Since the money I brought with me would run out soon, I knew I needed a job right away. Before I moved out of Levi's house, he told me about working at the Callan Park Hospital, which was one of the largest government-run mental hospitals in the country. He said it might work out well for me since the hospital's work schedule would allow me to travel. He explained that the hospital had two shifts and that the day shift was three 12-hour days with four days off, so I could make short trips to see the country. On the night shift, I could work five 12-hour nights, but then have an entire week off, enabling me to take a longer trip to explore Australia.

Being from Daytona Beach, I knew I wanted to be near the ocean and found out that Bondi Beach was the closest beach to Sydney. I managed to find a one-room flat on New Street, about a block away from the water for a reasonable price. The flat was like a one-room efficiency in the U.S., with a small refrigerator and stove, except that I wouldn't have my own private bathroom. I would have to share a bathroom and shower with the people from about five other flats. This was Australia's standard of living at the time, as their middle class was less well off than the middle class in America, and things were pretty costly there. The high cost of living was due to the island's geographic isolation. The country had to add a duty tax to cover import costs, and the average middle-class wage didn't go very far in a country with such high prices. Well, I wasn't happy about sharing a bathroom, but at least I would have my own place, I was close to the beach, and I wouldn't have to worry about being ripped off.

The Madhouse

NOW THAT I HAD MY HOUSING squared away, it was time to see about getting a job at the madhouse. I decided to take Levi's advice and check out Callan Park Mental Hospital since I didn't have any other leads. The hospital was in an area on the shores of Iron Cove in a Sydney suburb called Lilyfield. Now, when I say "hospital," don't think of a hospital by American standards, but more like an insane asylum in medieval times.

The part of the hospital above ground was built like a fortress in 1878. From 1878 to 1914, it had been called Callan Park Hospital for the Insane. It was constructed in an era when the profession of psychiatry was primitive at best and sadistic at worst: some of these mental patients were literally chained to the walls to prevent them from harming themselves or others. Callan Park Hospital had a bad reputation in the early 1900s, when it was notorious for staff physically abusing patients to control them.

During the early 1900s, having a mentally ill family member brought shame on the family name, so Callan Park had a method of bringing patients in by boat and running them through an underground tunnel to be admitted. At one time, all the wards were connected by these underground tunnels, but before I came to work there, the hospital sealed off the tunnels going to the different wards with concrete blocks. Now, since the tunnels had been sealed off, each ward had the equivalent of its own dungeon.

At one time, a stone wall ran along the perimeter of the hospital grounds, but now the walls were confined to each individual ward in an attempt to minimize the prison-like look of the place and seem more humane and progressive. The walls around each ward were about ten feet tall and were not constructed, needless to say, for decorative purposes.

Although I was a foreigner, getting hired at the hospital was not a problem for me. I didn't have to obtain a work visa (at least, I certainly don't remember getting one). And after six months of living in Australia, I simply had my travel visa extended another six months.

I was hired as a male nurse, but since I had no official training, I was assigned to the "backwards" at the rear of the hospital grounds. One ward was all female patients, one all male, and one was for all the patients with genetic abnormalities. Soon I would learn that these wards housed patients who were virtually incurable: no one got better and no one left. Basically, these wards just "warehoused" people. No family members came to visit them, no mental health treatment was received, and no one was ever discharged. They just wasted away there until they died.

Most of the clothing that these patients wore came from charitable contributions, so their personal wardrobe was less than basic. Patients wore a shirt, pants with no underwear, and shoes with no socks. In the foyer located near the door going out into the courtyard, a large box held donations of assorted clothes and shoes. When we noticed that a patient's clothes were soiled, torn, or extremely worn, a staff member would dig through the box to find something that would fit.

The patients were all given a drug called Largactil, used to treat various problems such as severe depression or behavioral disturbances. It came in a syrup form and was given to all the patients in the backwards three times a day with their meals. This drug helped keep patients calm and sedated as opposed to the old days of chaining them to the walls to keep them under control. One noticeable side effect of the Largactil was it made the skin sensitive to the sun, giving the patients' skin an odd orange tint, an outward sign of their outcast status.

The Motorcycle

WHEN I FIRST STARTED WORKING at the hospital, I took advantage of public transportation, catching two different buses to get to work each day. However, the public transportation was unionized, and they seemed to go on strike every other week. In fact, in the short time that I lived in Australia, the trains, buses, and cab drivers all went on strike, some time or another. Even the garbage pickup and funeral parlor workers went on strike.

I needed my own means of transport. But first I needed funds. I contacted my older brother Mike about the possibility of selling my car back in Daytona Beach for me. As I said before, it was a sweet 1969 Mach-1 Ford Mustang with 351HP, a sporty hood scoop, and three-speed on the floor. I hated to part with my beloved car, but I didn't have a choice.

I contacted Mike by mail since overseas phone calls were so expensive. It didn't take my brother long to sell it and mail me the money. After the balance owed on the car was paid off, I had enough profit to buy a motorcycle, which was cheaper and more fuel-efficient than a car.

There was just one kink in the plan to be the new owner of a motorcycle: I had no idea how to drive one! Thankfully, I had made friends with a colleague at the hospital named Antonio, and he agreed to teach me how to drive it. I decided to get a Honda 250 cc motorcycle because I heard they were reliable and would be good for a beginner like me. By American standards, this was a small bike, but in Australia, scooters and smaller bikes were more common due to the higher cost of gas.

Learning to drive a motorcycle was harder than I expected. Constantly, you are using both hands and both feet. You have a hand brake, a foot brake, a throttle, and a gear changer. I was always a good athlete and considered myself to be coordinated, but this took some getting used to. Like stopping a car on a hill with a clutch, you can dangerously roll backwards when starting from a stopped position! Well, much to my embarrassment, I learned that if you stop a motorcycle on a steep hill, you *must* apply *both* the hand brake *and* the foot brake, or you *will* roll backwards! Don't ask me how I found out!

Despite the initial struggles, after a while I gained confidence driving a motorcycle. I practiced driving late in the evening when the crowds had thinned out on Bondi Beach. I even got the hang of it well enough to stand on the seat and throttle the bike standing up!

Little did I know then that time would teach me a series of lessons of how invaluable a shield on your helmet, or a shield on your motorcycle, could be! As a novice, I was just trying to get by cheaply. But some things are worth paying for, or you will end up paying for it in other ways.

WARD B

Bart a.k.a. "Dummy"

THE FIRST WARD THAT I WORKED IN, and where I spent most of my eight months as a nurse, was Ward B, an all-male ward. Ward B contained 62 patients with an all-male staff. The staff consisted of one head nurse who remained inside the building while three other nurses supervised patients outside in the courtyard when the weather allowed. That was a lot of patients for such a small staff and would have been an impossible feat if we weren't instructed to give the patients sedatives three times daily with their meals.

To make matters worse, one of the staff members was required to manage one particular patient, --named Bart, at *all* times. That lucky staff member turned out to be me. Little did I know that my male nurse job would turn out to be more like a bouncer at a bar, breaking up fights all day over cigarettes! The required uniform for work was a gray shirt, gray pants, and a red neck tie. It didn't take me long to learn that I needed to quickly throw my tie over my shoulder to prevent the out-of-control patients from using it to choke me. Nor did I have a clue about how challenging my job would be trying to manage Bart while being distracted by breaking up fights!

For six of those eight months, I was responsible for keeping Bart from killing himself. No pressure there! Bart was a masochist, meaning a person who derives pleasure from inflicting pain on himself. Bart enjoyed pain to the extent that he tried to kill himself every chance he got. Bart was also deaf, never spoke a word, and had epilepsy. His arms bore many ugly scars from repeatedly breaking glass and cutting himself. More scar tissue ran from the neck down after he had set himself on fire on two different occasions in a suicide attempt. Bart was dangerous not only to himself. I was told that before I started working there, Bart had attacked another patient, bit off his ears, and ate them.

Evidently, Bart had a good mom who tried to raise him at home until he got too big to handle. In fact, she was the only relative who ever visited while I was at the hospital. But Bart was too much for even a devoted mother. The final straw was when he cut his own ears off with a razor blade and ate them.

* * *

Bart was one of five patients who had to be locked in confinement each night to protect himself and to protect other patients. Bart slept naked on the bare floor, covered only by a blue canvas tarp in the wintertime. The staff had tried to give Bart blankets and quilts to sleep with, but he always managed to tear them to shreds. In fact, he had even destroyed a series of mattresses and the tarp was the only thing strong enough to resist his destructive tendencies. The wooden floor in Bart's room had cracks between the boards that allowed cold air to creep in. Bitter cold air would blow in through the bars of his window since he had broken out the glass to cut himself.

These five "special" patients were put in their rooms naked, so they wouldn't use their clothes to hang themselves. The other four guys had sheets and blankets to cover themselves to sleep with, but Bart had only the blue tarp. The temperature got as cold as Atlanta in the winter and I could see my breath when I walked into his room in the mornings. You and I would be dead of pneumonia in a week if we had to sleep in the same conditions as Bart.

For almost every shift at the madhouse, I sat beside that joker in the courtyard just so he wouldn't kill himself. It didn't take me long to figure out that I was stuck with Bart because I was the "new kid on the block." No doubt, the other staff members laughed among themselves at having passed off this unwelcome responsibility onto me. I couldn't help but think of the song "Stuck in the Middle With You" by Stealers Wheel.

During those long shifts, since Bart never spoke, I thought about how frustrating, --to be incapable of communicating with anyone. I tried to rationalize why Bart would cut off his own ears and eat them. I thought maybe because he was deaf and upset that he couldn't hear. I wondered if pent up jealousy and anger drove Bart to bite off another person's ears, but to eat them *is* insanity. Finally, I realized that I needed to stop trying to explain his behavior rationally since I knew Bart was not of sound mind. I decided to nickname Bart "the Dummy" for all the crazy things he did on a regular basis. I realize now that such a nickname is not considered "politically correct"; however, during this time of my life, society was not concerned with political correctness. Many of my stories are centered around Bart. With all the time we spent together, Bart and I became best buds. In a manner of speaking...

WARD B

Toilet Seats

BART'S DESTRUCTIVE IMPULSES extended to the facilities as well. For whatever reason, Bart made a contest out of seeing how many toilet seats he could break before I caught him. The main bathroom on the first floor in Ward B was set up with five commodes sitting side by side, with no privacy dividers or doors. In addition, there was one commode for staff that had a privacy door that was kept locked.

Whenever I was distracted, Bart took advantage of the opportunity to make a beeline to the bathroom. Most days I managed to catch Bart before he got into the bathroom to do any damage. But some days, especially when I was busy breaking up fights, Bart would be free long enough to rip off toilet seats and bust them against the wall. On some days, he broke one or two, and, I hate to admit, on good days he would manage to get all five before I could get to him!

Anytime Bart got out of my sight, I ran for the bathroom in fearful anticipation of what was to come, bracing myself for that familiar sound of toilet lids breaking against the wall. BAM! There goes one! BAM! There goes two.... BAM! There goes three... As I would frantically run to stop him before he broke all five.

The staff commode privacy door did not extend all the way down to the floor, allowing Bart to crawl under it and get in. One day to my shame, Bart not only managed to break all five toilet seats, but he quickly crawled under the staff privacy door to get to the grand prize of the staff toilet lid. Before I could get the staff skeleton key out of my pocket to open the door to stop him, it was too late!

It was getting to the point that I was feeling sorry for the janitor having to replace the toilet seats. One day as I walked by, I heard him cussing after

Bart had made his rounds, and I heard him mumble under his breath, "Damn it! Why can't someone stop this nutcase from breaking these things!"

It made me feel ashamed that I couldn't do a better job of monitoring the Dummy. The janitor even dreamed up ways to intervene and thought of installing aluminum toilet lids that Bart might not be able to break. However, aluminum lids didn't work either, as Bart was able to dent them and bend them enough to create sharp edges on the seats, making them dangerous for use. Sad to say, but Bart was successful at least once a week in his daily ritual of seeing how many toilet seats he could break before I stopped him.

The Picnic

WARD B WAS AN ALL-MALE WARD and Ward C was an all-female ward. For whatever reason, the administration decided they wanted to have a picnic with the two wards together down by the river. They had food and even some music playing for entertainment and, surprisingly, everything went smoothly—for a while.

* * *

Even Bart was there. When they first mentioned having a picnic, I was sure he wouldn't be included. Why would anyone want to invite Bart to a picnic when he had cut off his own ears and eaten them, burnt himself at least two different times, and regularly cut himself with sharp objects? And yet, not only was he in attendance, but the night shift had failed to give him his necessary meds the night before.

The picnic went on for a while until suddenly, a scuffle broke out over cigarettes. I went to break up the fight and turned around only to see Bart running for the river. I could only assume he was planning to drown himself. Not wanting the death of a patient on my watch, I ran as fast as I could and mowed him down with a beautiful cross body block. I then walked him back to the picnic area and, forcefully, with both hands, set him down in the grass where most of the patients were seated.

This is where I screwed up. I sat down in front of Bart, facing him Indian-style, with my legs crossed under me. Bart was looking hard at my buttoned shirt pocket. To keep patients from stealing my wallet out of my back pants pocket, I had the habit of putting my wallet in my shirt pocket. To Bart, it must have looked like a pack of cigarettes, and where there are cigarettes there could be matches, and matches equal "fire!" The next thing I knew, Bart had grabbed me with both hands on my shirt and pulled me forward. I had absolutely no leverage as my legs were locked under me. Bart then ripped my shirt pocket open and saw that I had a wallet rather than cigarettes or matches.

But since he couldn't find matches to set himself on fire, he decided to bite my ears off. With his mouth wide open, Bart started mouthing my head, trying to locate my ears, as I yelled at the top of my lungs, "Get him off of me!" Thankfully, the staff was close by to come to my rescue and thank God with my hippie appearance, all Bart got was a mouthful of long hair!

Finally, the staff pulled him off me with a wad of my hair in his mouth, but then he really went crazy! He ripped all his clothes off and jerked off his shoes. In a rage, he began tearing his vinyl shoes to shreds with his teeth. I didn't know it was humanly possible to tear shoes apart, much less with one's teeth. He then threw his shoes down and began biting his forearms down to the bone. While this was going on, the head nurse ran to the hospital to get a shot to knock him out. Once administered, Bart was semi-conscious, and we dragged him back to the hospital. I'm thankful that at the time I had long hair and that I still have my ears!

No doubt, the average Joe would have quit a job like this, but I knew I would be working at the mental hospital for a short time since I had plans to eventually quit and travel the country. In the meantime, my goal was to work and save up money for traveling.

I knew the employee turnover rate was high; likely the reason I was hired and able to start to work immediately without any prior hospital experience or training. The personnel manager who hired me knew I was young and strong, and capable of handling male patients when they got aggressive. I guess that was enough for them.

On a typical day, after a long 12-hour shift, I would have to go straight home to rest up for the next day. By the time I got home, it was already dark. I had no time or energy for a social life outside of work until the end of my work week.

In the evenings, to save money, I would cook a quick and easy bachelor-type meal in the flat, such as baked chicken, hamburgers, or hot dogs. It turned out that having to share the shower and the toilet wasn't as much of a challenge as I originally thought it might be, since I was on a different shift than the other tenants in my flat.

The cost of living was so high that after paying my regular expenses, it was difficult to save much money. Nevertheless, I was looking forward to when I could quit this job and travel the country. That night as I lay exhausted in bed, although a maniac almost ate off my ears that day, I lost no sleep. It was the end of the work week, and I was looking forward to spending the next few days off at Bondi Beach.

WARD B

Tea Break from Hell

A S I SAID EARLIER, IN WARD B, the all-male staff was composed of one head nurse on the inside and three nurses in the courtyard supervising 62 patients. But when one nurse calls in sick and the patients don't get their nighttime medicine, life can get interesting.

* * *

To tell the story right, I need to tell you about the four main characters involved. First, there's Bart, "the Dummy," whom you already know. Then there's "Kim," a Chinese guy, who went around all day in the courtyard digging holes with a spade shovel and then filling them back up. Next, there's a patient whom I nicknamed "Road Runner." If you ever watched *The Road Runner Show* on TV, you know that he runs incredibly fast and can stop on a dime. The patient, Road Runner, had a daily habit of getting on the far side of the courtyard and running full speed directly toward me until, just when it seemed like he would crash full-force into me, he stopped suddenly, managing to not even touch me. When he abruptly stopped, he usually cleared his throat as if to cough up a loogie to spit on me. "Don't do that," I would tell him, shaking my finger. Of course, I wasn't sure how much Road Runner even understood, so frequently I would simply ignore him.

Finally, there was, "Bill," a patient who helped clean in Ward B. He was more right in the head than most of the other patients. However, this day, like all the other patients, he missed his meds and didn't have it together either.

Now there were only two of us staff members monitoring the courtyard and my co-worker went on his 15-minute tea break, --equivalent to the American coffee break. That leaves me alone with the 62 mental patients, one of whom (the Dummy) must be watched nonstop. Let the fun begin!

* * *

It was summertime, and an extended drought had left the landscape parched and dusty. The grass was dry in the courtyard and a discarded cigarette butt started a grass fire. There was one patient asleep in the grass, like a dog lying in the sun. A light wind started blowing the fire right toward him. Bart, the Dummy, spots the fire and wants to try again to burn himself to death. Immediately, I grabbed him by his shirt and held him back from the fire.

At that moment, Bill was walking by, and since he was usually "helpful," I yelled to him, "Wake him up! Wake him up!" I needed to get the sleeping patient out of the path of the fire.

Next thing I know, Bill is standing over the guy punching him in the face yelling, "Wake up! Wake up!" This poor innocent patient now lay unconscious in a pool of blood. While having to continuously hold Bart by his shirt, I grabbed the previously sleeping, now "unconscious" patient by his foot and pulled him down the grassy slope of the hill to get him out of the path of the approaching flames.

About that time, Kim came by with his spade shovel, and I got the wise idea of using his shovel to put out the fire. Naturally, knowing that Kim never went anywhere without his prized spade shovel, when I forced it from his tight grasp, Kim got extremely upset and started cussing me out in Chinese! Kim wanted his shovel back! Miraculously, I somehow managed to resist Kim's physical advances and tirade of profanity to use his spade to put out the fire. Of course, this was an incredible feat performed while dodging Kim's aggressive attempts to retrieve his shovel and tightly holding onto Bart to prevent him from jumping into the spreading fire.

Now that the fire was out and feeling quite aggravated, I took Bart and shoved him back into his chair. Every day I sat by Bart in a chair in the courtyard to make sure he didn't kill himself. As soon as I sat down, a fight broke out over cigarettes—an almost daily occurrence there. Mental patients would try to steal cigarettes from other patients, inevitably ending in violence.

In the process of breaking up the fight, I turned around to monitor Bart and, noticing his empty chair, scanned the courtyard just as he was clearing the first tier of the building. Bart had taken advantage of my absence to climb up the three tiers of the building in the courtyard in order to take a swan dive off the roof. I ran and caught up with Bart just as he was clearing the third floor, grabbed him by the pants, and pulled him down. Then I marched Bart back to his chair and, more aggravated than ever, pushed him down into it and sat beside him.

Taking a deep breath, I looked across the courtyard. Now the Road Runner was ripping off his clothes until he was butt naked. Suddenly, he charged at me, like he routinely did; however, this time, since he hadn't gotten his nightly medication, he failed to stop, knocking me over backwards in my chair, causing my sunglasses to go flying. As I got back up, he started whaling at me, swinging his arms like a girl and hitting me.

Since the Road Runner was naked, I really didn't want to punch him or grab him to make him stop, so all I could think of was to kick him between the legs. Surprised that my first kick didn't even get a reaction, I kicked him a second time. This time I simply got an "Ughh," and then he turned and ran off to the other side of the courtyard. About that time, the other male nurse came back from his 15-minute tea break. I didn't say a word about what took place during his absence. I was much too aggravated to even discuss it. Just another fun day at the madhouse!

One Good Turn Deserves Another

WONDERING ABOUT WHY the patients periodically were not getting their medications on the night shift, I concluded that Greg, the hippie-type, long-haired male head nurse was stealing the meds to sell or use, or both. This would explain the fiasco during the picnic and the tea break from hell when the patients had not been given their meds the night before.

I know it wasn't right, but as reprisal, the other day shift guys and I decided to get back at the night shift by getting the patients all stirred up before the night shift showed up. The day shift staff was responsible for putting the patients to bed before the night shift came in. We knew that a lot of the patients were peculiarly particular about their beds. For example, one patient's bed had about a one-foot gap between the top mattress and the box springs where he had been stashing and hording newspapers, magazines, and other personal objects. Another patient had a thing for keeping his bed extremely neat, military- style, with the sheets and blankets all pulled tight without a wrinkle to be found.

To rile up the patients, we went about messing up the some of these patients' beds, throwing pillows on the floor, pulling sheets and blankets off the beds, and pulling out the stashes of papers and magazines sandwiched in between the mattresses. Obviously, the patients were not happy, especially the patient who found his prized collection of treasures dumped out onto the floor. I'm sure the night shift had a rough night, but I bet it would never compare to my "tea break from hell!" Now I know that what we did back then was wrong, but at the time, "one good turn deserves another."

WARD B

Cookie Monster

ANOTHER PATIENT IN WARD B whom I dealt with often was Sammie. This guy was only about five feet tall and truly ugly. Sammie always walked around clenching a wad of torn up rags with a death grip in his left hand. These shredded rags dangled like streamers held in an upright position with his arm bent at the elbow. It was apparent that Sammie treasured the rags like a security blanket, showing them off with pride.

It wasn't long before I learned that Sammie had a bad habit of going around pinching everyone, patients and staff included, on the back of their upper arms—hard enough to leave black and blue marks. Sammie managed to pinch me on my very first day on the job, but I came up with a plan to make sure it was the last time!

* * *

Remember, the patients did not wear belts, and they never wore underwear under their clothes. So, I searched in the hospital's donation box and found him a pair of oversized pants. Since Sammie's left hand was always clinging fiercely to his security rags, I came up with the idea of giving him extra baggy pants to wear so he would have to use his free right hand to hold them up. Thank goodness, keeping both of Sammie's hands busy seemed to resolve the pinching problem. Now he was basically harmless.

Sammie's whole life revolved around food—the reason why I nicknamed him "Cookie Monster." He spoke very few words and would mostly just grunt and groan. However, there were two short sentences that he would occasionally say in his extremely low rough and gruff voice. The most common was, "I want a loaf of bread!" and the other was, "I want a woman!" I asked Sammie one time, if he could have his choice between a loaf of bread or a woman, which would he rather have? He sat there for a few moments; the wheels were slowly turning in his head as he carefully contemplated this most complex question. Finally, after a long pause, Sammie replied, "A loaf of bread!" Needless to say, I laughed 'til I cried at his response!

As Sammie was restricted to an all-male ward, I often wondered how he would react if he *was* around a woman. One day, some female nurses came to Ward B for a day of training and I was amused to observe Sammie following the women around all day. Frequently, he would harmlessly go up to smell perfume on their shoulders.

Five of the patients, including Sammie, had to eat their food outside in the courtyard because they were too uncivilized in their habits to eat in the dining room with everyone else. Sammie would devour his food in about five seconds, then hold his plate up to his face and rapidly lick it hard with his tongue from top to bottom, almost smacking himself in the face with his plate. Then he would be ready to devour the other four patients' food. I had to stand with my arm outstretched and my hand on his forehead, stiff-arming him to keep him at bay. My hand was on his forehead rather than his chest because, although I was only five foot six, I was tall compared to Sammie.

Sammie wasn't allowed into the dining room mainly to prevent him from eating the other patients' food. Before dinner, each table was set up with a large loaf of sliced bread and a dish of butter. The daily meal routine at the madhouse was to have all the male patients line up single file to enter through one main door of the dining room. The fact that Sammie was short made it easy for him to make a game out of trying to weasel himself toward the front of the line to be the first through the door, then run to grab up one of the full loaves of sliced bread. It was a challenge for Sammie to grip one end of the loaf with the hand still holding his torn rags and then use his other hand to grab the other end of the loaf. Desperately trying to hold the slices together, occasionally losing a few pieces, he would immediately try to devour all of the bread in his hands before we took it away from him.

On one occasion, as luck would have it, on a day Sammie managed to sneak into the dining area, there was a new young cafeteria lady in the kitchen. Just as I came through the doorway, I noticed Sammie several tables away anxiously and greedily eyeing a loaf of bread. He stood frozen in thought, trying to figure out how to grab the bread while both hands were occupied, having to hold up his baggy pants with his right and his rags in his left.

Sammie decided for the loaf of bread over the pants. His pants fell to the floor as he scooped up the bread and there he stood butt naked, waist down, before the lunch lady. "Get him out of here! He's disgusting!" she hollered. The new lunch lady got broken in right on her first day!

In addition to Bart, Sammie was another one of the five patients who were required to be locked up at night. I wasn't sure why he needed to be in confinement when he was virtually harmless, but assumed it may have been due to his child-like curiosity. He probably had a bad habit of getting into people's personal belongings during the night.

Interestingly, Sammie turned out to be my favorite patient. Again, to me, he was harmless, other than pinching people, and as I mentioned earlier, I had taken care of that. I was amused by how much he savored everything he ate, and I would watch as he closed his eyes in a state of ecstasy as he devoured his food. When I worked the night shift I would often go to his room to give him a treat. Sammie always slept with his sheet pulled up over his head and would hear me unlocking his door with the skeleton key. Routinely, he would cry out in his low gruff voice, "Out of my room!"

One night as I stood holding a nice big juicy apple behind my back to surprise him, I replied, "But Sammie, I have something for you!" At this, he quickly pulled his sheet down and I handed him the apple, which he took eagerly and immediately covered his head back up.

Then I waited. Next, just like the Cookie Monster that he was, loud crunching sounds came from beneath the sheet as he devoured the apple as fast as he could. Knowing Sammie was harmless, sometimes I would pull back his sheet just to catch a glimpse of his face. He would be lying in bed, with his head propped up with a pillow and with his eyes shut, juice running down his face onto to his bare chest—chewing away. Eating was, no doubt, his thing. Sammie was in hog heaven!

The Night Shift

WHILE WORKING THE NIGHT SHIFT in Ward B, some of the male nurses showed me some of the tricks of the trade. During the long 12-hour shift from 6:30 p.m. to 6:30 a.m., the staff was supposed to make an hourly walk through the ward to make sure the patients were sleeping and not "up to no good." Of course, none of us did the "walk through" hourly as we were supposed to. Usually we just put a mattress on the floor in a utility room, located just inside the entrance door of the upstairs ward, and slept there most of the night.

I regularly locked myself in the utility room, and I had one of the patients (an early riser) knock on my door and wake me before the morning shift came in. As a backup in case a night supervisor came by to check on the ward, I learned a trick using a coat hanger as an early warning system. I cut off the top curved part of a hanger and bent it tighter to make it fit into the keyhole from the inside of the main door to the upstairs patients' sleeping ward. This kept the night supervisor from being able to turn their key and unlock the door.

One night this trick actually saved me. Sound asleep in the utility room, I was suddenly awakened by the sound of the night supervisor fumbling to get his key in the lock. Then he started banging on the outside main entry door in frustration. In the commotion, I jumped up, ran from my room over to the door, and smoothly slipped the coat hanger wire out of the lock with my left hand as I slipped the skeleton key in with my right hand and opened the door to the upstairs sleeping area. The supervisor commented that he didn't know what the problem was with the locks in the different wards. Funny, I never knew if the trouble he had been experiencing in the other wards was from other staff members pulling the same trick.

I was fortunate that none of the patients passed away in their sleep during the nights while I was sleeping on the job. Obviously, if someone died six hours before you reported it, the body would be stone cold. You would have a lot of questions to answer about whether you had been doing your job and making your hourly routine walk through. Some of the male nurses shared another trick in this scenario. To help "cover your butt," they suggested bathing the cold dead body in warm water, drying them off, and redressing them to throw off the authorities on the time of death. I was so glad I never had to deal with such a situation!

WARD B

Fun in the Dungeon

THE DUNGEONS AT CALLAN PARK Hospital ended up being a place of escape from the madness around us. They were also where most of the male staff members went to smoke pot. Smoking enabled us to laugh about our job situation rather than be depressed. It's a good thing the administration didn't know what all went on down in the dungeons.

* * *

The kitchen lady who had the awkward encounter with Sammie didn't last long, and soon a new girl replaced her. She was considerably overweight but had a pretty face. On her first day of work, the head male nurse, Greg, and two other male nurses talked her into going down into the dungeon and having sex. There were no beds, no mattresses; just a cold, damp, dirty stone floor in utter darkness, so standing up and leaning up against the stone wall was the easiest option.

The guys figured they could get away with not attending their patients long enough for sex, as long as I was keeping an eye on Bart. Since I had been out in the courtyard, I didn't learn about this until after the fact. I would not have been interested in joining the guys in this indiscriminate escapade anyway, since she was too loose and too overweight to be appealing to me. I can only wonder what this girl replied when her mother asked her later that day, "How was your first day on the job, dear?" Having sex with three strangers in a dungeon on Day 1 is pretty noteworthy—not that you'd want to tell your mom about it.

Outside the walls of the Callan Park Hospital, rumors circulated about the dungeons under the wards, and many people were curious to see them.

The head male nurse, Greg, was like a fox in the henhouse. As I mentioned earlier, he was a long-haired hippie type who used and sold drugs on the hospital grounds, and he definitely wasn't above breaking any of the hospital rules.

While working the night shift, Greg got a call from his best friend who wanted to bring his girlfriend to see the dungeons. Bringing in outside people into the wards was one of the strictest rules that we knew not to break, mainly because administration was worried about people taking pictures of the patients or of the conditions of the facility. There was no doubt that getting caught breaking this rule would be grounds for immediate termination. But Greg, like me, not afraid of living on the edge, arranged for his friends to come.

While Greg and I were waiting on the young couple to show up, we decided to play a little trick on them using Sammie. I went up to Sammie's room, unlocked the door, and got my usual nightly greeting from him.

"Out of my room!" he shouted.

"But Sammie, I've got something for you!" I said. This time, instead of a nice green apple, I had a loaf of bread to tempt him. I gave him one slice of bread, which he took eagerly, then another, and another, one by one to lure him out of the room and down the hallway. Of course, he wasn't wearing any clothes—Sammie slept naked, like all the patients locked in individual rooms at night.

* * *

I led him from his room on the second floor down the stairwell to the first floor, where I met Greg at the dungeon entrance.

"Do you have a torch?" Greg said.

Picturing a thick stick with a flame at the end, I didn't know where I could have gotten a torch or why he would ask if I had. "No," I said.

"Take this," he replied and handed me a flashlight. (I chuckled under my breath.) That was when I learned that in Australia, they call a flashlight a "torch."

The dungeon was below ground level and its absence of windows made it so dark that you couldn't even see your hand in front of your face. Shining the way, I led the naked Sammie down the dark, spiral stone stairwell, like something from a castle in medieval times. The bottom of the stairwell opened up into a massive pitch-black room the size of the entire ward above. This large room had a few small side rooms where I took Sammie and waited for the young couple to come down the stairs. To keep Sammie occupied and happy, I was continually feeding him slices of bread, one at a time.

The couple thought that they were going to get a tour of the dungeon, but our plan was to lock them in the dungeon with Sammie. As I thought about what was about to happen, I began laughing to myself so hard I was crying.

The turn of the lock upstairs signaled that Greg had arrived. A shaft of light poured in from the opened door above. I would love to have been able to see this couple and watch the expression on their faces as they entered the dungeon, but the spiral staircase hid them from my sight. Greg gave the couple a flashlight (that was *not* turned on) and surprised them by pushing the old wooden door shut and locking it with the skeleton key. Then I heard a deep gasp. The couple were suddenly standing in a vastness of utter darkness. As they banged on the locked door, the guy frantically yelled, "What the hell, Greg! Why'd you lock the freaking door? You said you were going to give us a tour!"

There was dead silence from the other side of the door. Greg did not respond. I heard some commotion as the startled couple struggled to turn on their flashlight.

They beat on the door again and shouted to get back out, but that was not part of our plan. When the couple realized Greg was *not* going to let them out, the guy told his girlfriend, "We came all this way to see the dungeon, so we might as well look around." As I watched the light from their flashlight get closer and closer as they descended the stairs, I tried hard to contain my laughter. Then I gave Sammie what was left of the bag of bread and quietly shoved the very ugly, naked Sammie (with the appearance not quite as scary, but very similar to "Gollum" in *Lord of the Rings)*, out of the side room into the massive black abyss.

The couple swung the beam of the light across the cold stone surface as they cautiously explored. "What was that?" the guy said suddenly. "I saw something out of the corner of my eye! Did you see it?"

"I didn't see anything. What was it?" his girlfriend said nervously.

The next thing I heard was a loud "Ugh!" from Sammie when the light must have shined in his face. Sammie squinted as he stood butt naked, holding up his rags in his left hand and his bag of bread in his right hand.

"Oh, shit!" the boyfriend yelled, as his girlfriend let out a blood curdling scream. They ran back up the stairwell and beat on the door, desperately hollering, "Let us out! Let us out!" I thought they were going to beat the door off the hinges before Greg could unlock the door and let them back out into the light.

I retrieved Sammie and returned him to his room. Then I went back to see Greg. By the time I got back to talk with him about the night's events, the couple had already left. I never did get to meet the couple, but I'm sure I helped warp them for life. Just another fun night at the madhouse!

WARD C

Grabbing Hold of a Bobcat

WARD C, THE ALL-FEMALE WARD, was the counterpart of Ward B. During my eight months at the hospital, I probably spent only two days in the female ward, and only when the ward was short-handed when a staff member called in sick. On my first day there, a female nurse showed me around the ward and familiarized me with the different patients. As we were walking around, we passed an old woman sitting in a chair masturbating. The nurse said, "Don't mind her, she pleasures herself several times a day." I saw another female patient who must have weighed over three hundred pounds and had an almost full beard. The nurse said this woman had been admitted for choking two people to death. We walked on, until I spotted an older Jewish woman with tattooed numbers on her forearm from her days in a concentration camp as a child. I thought it was really sad that she had survived the concentration camp only to end up in another hellhole like this.

* * *

Then the nurse introduced me to Maggie, who was always locked up in a single room overnight. This woman was in her sixties and was small, wiry, and very skinny. The nurse told me that Maggie wasn't exactly a "morning person" because when you first unlocked her door in the mornings to let her out of her room, she had the habit of throwing her filled bedpan at you as her morning greeting.

On my second morning in the female ward, at about 6:30, I was to unlock Maggie's door. I hadn't even had my first cup of tea, but, I thought to myself, "I've got this; I know her morning ritual. All I have to do is unlock her door and step away as I fling the door open."

Everything went according to plan as the bed pan came flying out the door, splattering urine and feces on the floor. I thought to myself, *HAHA, MISSED ME!* But then: *OOPS! Here she comes!* Maggie came running out of the room full speed, screaming and flailing her arms violently. She clawed, kicked, and tried to bite me as I struggled to keep her off me, but it was like trying to grab hold of a bobcat. Although this woman was old and tiny, it was all I could do to hold her down.

Suddenly, her hand shot out and she grabbed my tie as tightly as Sammie clung to his rags, then moved like she was going to choke me with it. It all happened so quickly, I didn't have time to throw my tie over my shoulder in an attempt to protect myself—a trick I had learned from previous encounters in other wards.

Alerted by all the noise, the female nurses hurriedly came to my aid. Together, we contained Maggie and put her back in her room. I didn't like having to manhandle an elderly woman, even if she, obviously, wasn't the sweet grandmotherly type. I was glad I only had to spend two days in the female ward.

WARD C

The Queen's Birthday

ONE BRIGHT, SUNNY AFTERNOON, the kind Sydney is famous for, I decided to go body surfing. Since Bondi Beach was only a block from my flat, on my days off, I often made the short walk down New Street to the beach—a much-needed break from the chaos of the madhouse. At the time, the beachfront was less developed than it is now.

Approaching the beach, I quickly noticed that there was a larger gathering than normal. I asked someone in the crowd what was going on, and he told me it was the Queen of England's birthday. Being from America, I didn't know Australia celebrated Queen Elizabeth II's birthday as a holiday. This holiday turned out to be a big beach event where lifeguards came from all over the country for water competitions.

* * *

The beach was in a U-shaped cove with jetties on each side. There was a grassy area and a short stone wall with a stairway leading down to the sandy shore. As I approached the beach, I climbed up on the stone wall to get a bird's eye view of the cove where all the activity was happening. As luck would have it, the waves turned out to be twenty feet tall, the biggest waves that I saw my entire time in Australia! I was eager to body surf such great waves, but was disappointed to find out that no one was allowed to even go in the water that day because of the competitions. Nevertheless, I decided to stick around and observe. From my perch on the wall, I heard the spectators let out a big, "Ohhhh!" As I strained to see what the noise was all about, I spotted a large wooden row boat with six men paddling for their lives in a desperate attempt to clear an enormous wave. The massive wave flipped them over backwards and the boat exploded into splinters as it hit the huge boulders on the shoreline!

Another "Ohhhh!" went up from the crowd as a second wooden boat collided dangerously into the large boulders, flipping over backwards and exploding into pieces! Now splinters of wood and people bobbed around in the foaming surf like corks. Next, two men cranked up a really nice fiberglass speedboat equipped with two massive engines. Surely, I thought, a speed boat would clear the waves better than the wooden boats. Not so. In no time, I saw the speed boat flip backwards, slam against the huge wall of rock, and bust into a million pieces.

At this point, another beachgoer filled me in on what was happening. He told me that before I arrived, a group of people had parachuted out of an airplane. All of them were supposed to land on the beach, but one woman, unfortunately, landed in the water. Every time a big wave came into shore, it would pull her parachute down under the water and her with it. All the boats were attempting to rescue the drowning woman.

Finally, some of the lifeguards avoided the big waves by taking advantage of the jetty and successfully approached the woman from behind the surf. They proceeded to bring her ashore right below where I was standing on the wall and desperately performed CPR on her until an ambulance arrived. Sadly, I learned later that she had taken on too much water and did not survive. Such a tragedy that the girl had to drown with the number of boats available for rescue, not to mention a beach full of lifeguards!

WARD D

Broke in Right

WARD D WAS FOR THE CRIMINALLY insane and was a terrifying place. Just about everybody in the ward was a sexual predator or had committed murder—or multiple murders. Ironically, this ward housed some of the saner patients in the facility. They had good attorneys who managed to get them out of doing time in a hard-core prison by having them committed to a mental hospital.

This was a maximum-security ward that was so thorough in its safety procedures that we even had to count the silverware after each meal to make sure the patients didn't steal them to use as weapons later. To this day, I wonder why the hospital didn't just simply use plasticware, which would have been safer and probably less expensive considering the time spent counting silverware before anyone could leave the cafeteria.

As I was monitoring patients going through the lunch line, a patient named Peter, overweight and standing about five feet, ten inches tall, brought his tray of food to the table near me and sat down. About that time another patient named Jim, who was about six feet, two inches tall and muscular, walked by Peter's table and rudely shouted, "What'd you say to me?"

Peter hadn't said anything and was just sitting there, minding his business and eating his meal. The next thing I knew, Jim attacked the severely overmatched Peter, knocking him down to the floor and pounded him mercilessly. Two older male nurses just stood together off to the side in full view of the fight. Being new in this ward, I looked over at them for some help or guidance as to what I should do, but was surprised as they just stood there calmly with their arms folded, watching Jim beat up Peter. I figured something must be up.

Jim continued to hit Peter until he was knocked out in a pool of blood. The two nurses walked over and asked Jim if he was okay. He answered, "Yes," and they took him to the office to doctor his hands and left Peter unconscious on the floor. Thankfully, a young male nurse came to the aid of Peter, and I crouched down to assist him. Soon, Peter gained consciousness and we helped him back to his feet and back to his single room where we helped clean him up.

Curious about what just happened, after leaving Peter's room, I learned from the young male nurse that the older guys had it in for Peter. They had made plans for Jim to beat him up for what he had done to his mother. Peter was in the hospital for raping his own mother and stabbing her to death with a screwdriver. These two nurses had made a deal with Jim, who, I learned, had been a mafia enforcer. Jim was the guy who came and broke your arms and legs if you didn't pay your debt. He was a bad dude who was skilled in karate and other ways of harming people—all in all, a man you would not want to mess with. Jim was one of the sane cases I mentioned before; one of those guys whose lawyers weaseled them out of a prison sentence, so they could do their time in a mental hospital.

The two older male nurses I found out worked in Ward D all the time. These two men, in their fifties, were not shifted from ward to ward like the other staff, perhaps because they were older and had gotten established with the administration as well as with their patients. In the short time that I worked in this ward, it had become apparent that these two were thoroughly corrupt. They showed favoritism and exploited for personal gain, such as making patients wash their cars. These two male nurses used bribes such as extra food at mealtime and staying up later to watch television at night to get patients like Jim to do whatever they wanted. They were bad to deal out cruel and unconventional physical punishment. On my first day in Ward D, I learned they played "hardball."

Ben

ANOTHER INTERESTING PATIENT in Ward D was Ben. One day I was sitting outside in the courtyard watching the other patients when Ben pulled up a chair beside me and started talking like he had known me all his life. It was obvious he had some personality about him as he started his first conversion by saying, "Pretty crazy place to work, huh?"

"You got that right!" I replied.

Ben continued, "So what got you working in a shithole like this?"

Catching me off guard, I had to bite my lip to keep from laughing. But I kept my composure and said, "I moved here recently from America and needed a job."

"Where from in America?"

"Daytona Beach, Florida," I said.

"Oh, really! I watch the Daytona races on TV in Australia!" Ben said excitedly. "I'm a big racing fan!"

We had other interesting discussions about the Vietnam War and the racial riots in America. We carried on varied conversations for almost a week and unlike most mental patients, Ben's mind never seemed to wander. He seemed so normal.

Finally, I asked another male nurse what Ben was in the hospital for. It turned out that dear old Ben was an actual AXE MURDERER! The story went that he murdered his wife with an axe and mailed her various body parts to her relatives.

One day I was shopping in a department store in downtown Sydney when I heard someone say, "Hi, Pat!" I looked up and it was Ben! My immediate thoughts were to jump on him, wondering if he had escaped from the Callan Park Mental Hospital. Ben's demeanor was relaxed, and I realized he was merely out shopping for clothes just like I was, so I quickly collected myself. We carried on a short conversation and then went our separate ways. As I left the store, I was wondering what people would have thought if they knew they were out shopping next to an axe murderer.

When I returned to the hospital, I started asking questions, extremely curious to know why in the world Ben was outside the hospital walls. I was told that he had permission to leave the grounds for a few hours once a week. The hospital's psychiatrist had determined that Ben was not a danger to the public, but only to his wife—and he had already taken care of her.

Steve

STEVE WAS YOUNGER THAN MOST people in Ward D. He was in his twenties and of average height and weight. His admission to the hospital was due his drug and alcohol abuse combined with his schizophrenic-like personality. Staff said he had a problem where he heard voices that told him to do things he shouldn't do, such as stab a man to death on the sidewalk whom he had never met. When I was off duty, Steve attacked a male nurse and used the nurse's key to escape the hospital grounds. It was wintertime, and since Steve got cold and wet trying to survive the outdoors, he went to the local hospital and complained of phony ailments to get checked in for a warm bed and meals. Taking full advantage of Australia's socialized medical system, he spent three days undergoing medical tests for his made-up ailments. After three days of this, the hospital concluded that Steve probably had some mental issues and called Callan Park Hospital to see if they were missing a patient.

My next day on duty, the administration of Callan Park Hospital had me and another male nurse go to the local general hospital to pick up Steve to return him to Ward D. When Steve saw us arrive, his eyes grew wide with fear. We drove Steve back to Callan Park Hospital using no restraints and without incident. Normally he would have been housed with the general population in Ward D, but as punishment, I was directed to lock Steve up in a single room for the night.

Twelve hours later, on my next shift, when I was instructed to let Steve out of his confined room, I noticed that he had two black eyes. I concluded that some members of the staff had paid him a visit during the night to beat him up as a lesson for attacking a staff member. Like I said before, they played hardball in Ward D.

Jack a.k.a. Hannibal Lecter

THE MOST DANGEROUS and the scariest of the patients in Ward D was Jack. Jack was in his thirties and at more than six feet tall and 200 pounds, he was a strikingly intimidating figure. His violent nature, along with his size and age, made him a force to be reckoned with. Jack was a kind of real-life Hannibal Lecter, the fictional serial killer in the movie *The Silence of the Lambs,* played by the renowned actor Anthony Hopkins. Like Hannibal, Jack had committed multiple murders and was just waiting on his chance to murder you.

Before I came to work at the mental hospital, Jack once grabbed a pen out of a staff member's pocket and stabbed him in the eye, blinding him. Over twenty-three hours of every day, Jack was locked up in isolation and only allowed out for one hour. But, in reality, Jack was only released for a few minutes once a day, simply to walk up and down the hallway. Unless four male nurses were there to guard him, his door was never unlocked.

Largactil, the most commonly used drug to treat patients in psychiatric hospitals worldwide, including patients with schizophrenia and psychosis, was given out in liquid form three times a day with meals. Most patients were given a shot glass-sized dose, equivalent to two tablespoons or one ounce, three times a day with their meals. Jack's regular dosage was a *full eight-ounce glass* three times a day and he was *still* violent and difficult to control! Fortunately, I never saw Jack go off, and I'm really glad I never had to help subdue him. Knowing how dangerous Jack and many of the other patients were in Ward D, I'm thankful that I spent little time there.

WARD F

Ooooh That Smell…

THE MADHOUSE ROUTINELY moved nurses and other staff from ward to ward to prevent burnout. Each ward had its own unique kind of hell to offer or experience. Once again, I got broken in right on my first day in a new ward—the unbearable, hopeless Ward F.

Ward F was an all-male ward that housed patients with a variety of genetic defects. On my first day in the ward, it was pouring down rain, so no one could be in the courtyard which unfortunately meant all patients were confined to indoors. Everyone was stuck inside a large empty room containing nothing but a TV mounted out of reach in one corner. There wasn't even any furniture.

As the male head nurse, who was showing me around the ward, unlocked the door to the TV room with his skeleton key, the first thing that hit me was the reeking, overpowering smell of shit! Reluctantly, I entered the room to see piles of human feces everywhere and streaks of brown on the walls. The patients had finger-painted all over the walls with crap. I almost barfed from the odor and was scared to even take a step or lean up against the walls. The head nurse told me it could have been worse—six months earlier, all the patients' feces had worms in it, and it was quite an undertaking for the hospital to rid the patients of worms. Well, today we only had to contend with wormless shit—*lucky me!* I started thinking that my old job at Delta Airlines wasn't looking so bad right about now.

Wondering what I had gotten myself into and whether I could tolerate such shitty working conditions, literally, I knew that other staff members had put up with the crappy, gross, disgusting parts of this job, and hopefully, so could I—at least for a short amount of time.

Peas, Carrots, and Corn

ANOTHER PICTURE-PERFECT Kodak moment in Ward F happened when I was outside in the courtyard monitoring several patients who were too unruly to eat in the cafeteria with the others. It was a nice, sunny day, and I had brought a sack lunch with a couple sandwiches and a Coke to enjoy outdoors. As I sat down and started eating, all the other patients began filing out of the cafeteria into the courtyard. One of these patients wandered over to me and proceeded to vomit an undigested pile of peas, carrots, and corn at my feet. As if that wasn't bad enough, three of the other patients quickly ran over and began eating the vegetables out of his vomit. *Welcome to my world!* I suppose the patient that threw up had eaten his food much too fast and perhaps the intense heat of the outdoors got to him. Thanks to my gross experiences working in Ward F, to this very day, I like to tell people that I could eat spaghetti at an autopsy and it would not bother me.

Charlie

ANOTHER PATIENT IN WARD F who has not escaped my memory is Charlie. Tall and skinny, Charlie, like many of the other patients, lived to eat. The courtyard in Ward F was surrounded by a six-foot-tall chain link fence topped with three intimidating strands of barbed wire. During my first week in Ward F when we were outside in the courtyard, out of the corner of my eye, I saw Charlie step on the side of the fence and hurtle up over the top. He easily cleared all three strands of barbed wire, as effortlessly as a gazelle.

Since it was the first time I had a patient escape, I quickly looked over at the head male nurse and asked what we should do. He nonchalantly responded, "Don't worry; I know where Charlie is going."

Knowing the patients in our ward were being watched by other staff members, the head nurse took me outside the courtyard to the next ward. There was Charlie, a short distance down the hill from us, eating out of the dumpster! Evidently, this was a fairly common practice for him. His escape routine happened about twice a week, and when it did, I knew I could find Charlie in the dumpster.

One day after Charlie went missing, I went to the dumpster to retrieve him but was alarmed to see he wasn't there! I had no idea what to do, so I went back to the ward and told the head nurse. This time, a look of panic flashed across the head nurse's face. "Oh, no!" he said. "I think I know where he's gone."

On the far side of the hospital grounds, acres away from the wards, was an Italian bakery. As I mentioned earlier, originally there had been a big wall around the entire hospital premises, but in an attempt to make Callan Park Hospital look less like a prison, the wall had been removed.

Currently, only each individual ward was surrounded by fencing. This made it pretty easy to leave the grounds in the rare instance when a patient managed to escape from his respective ward.

We walked the long distance to the bakery and had just gotten to the entrance when Charlie came bursting out the front door with a long loaf of French bread in his mouth, several loaves of bread under one arm, and a decorated birthday cake squished up under the other arm. The owner, a stereotypical-looking Italian baker, heavyset with a mustache, dark hair, and a white chef's hat, sprung through the door after Charlie. When the chef saw us, he began ranting and raving, waving his arms and shaking his fist and gesturing in that very Italian way as he cussed us out in Italian.

Unable to communicate properly with the chef, we just left with Charlie to take him back to his ward. I assumed this had probably happened more than once and that the hospital must have made good on the damage Charlie caused at the bakery.

In addition to being extremely athletic, Charlie had a unique ability to toss a coin in his hand like no one I've ever seen. He would take a coin about the size of a quarter, cup his hand, and toss it on its edge, rolling it around and round like a juggler. Charlie was so coordinated that he would walk around tossing his coin vertically like there was nothing to it. He did this without even looking at the coin, as if it were a natural reflex for him, as effortless as blinking your eyes.

The director of Callan Park Hospital lived on the hospital grounds, at the bottom of a hill that sloped down from Ward F. The director was also the head psychiatrist, a well-educated man with three different degrees. One day he showed up unannounced to visit Charlie's ward. This was my first time seeing the director. He was middle-aged, wore a suit, and looked quite sophisticated. I came around a corner in Ward F only to catch him by surprise trying to copy Charlie's unique coin trick. Glancing up at me, the director immediately turned several shades of red from embarrassment. Definitely an awkward moment, but neither of us spoke a word as I continued down the hall. I thought it was extremely funny that a man so educated could not duplicate the coin trick of Charlie, who probably had the IQ of a monkey.

Charlie usually didn't talk much. In fact, he was more like a parrot in that he would only repeat catch phrases that he heard people say. Usually he uttered no more than two words at a time—if he said anything at all.

One day I noticed Charlie next to the chain link fence, his fingers gripping onto the wire as he gazed intently at the other side. "Oh, no!" I thought. "He's getting ready to jump the fence again." All of a sudden, Charlie totally went off, violently shaking the fence and yelling, "F--- you! F--- you!" over and over again!

I ran over to the fence to see who or what he was shouting at. Down the hill, directly below the courtyard, stood the director's house in plain view. The yard was set up with tables covered with crisp white linens and decorated with candles and flowers—a romantic setting in the cool of the evening; at least romantic prior to Charlie's rude, crude outburst.

The director was having an outdoor party for his friends prior to attending the opera. His male guests were dressed in tuxedos and the women in fine evening gowns. "F--- you! F--- you!" yelled Charlie. As Charlie continued his raving verbal assault, the guests looked up toward him and began to retreat into the house. Quickly, I pulled Charlie off the fence and took him inside to calm him down.

It wasn't any surprise to me that Charlie was soon moved to another ward, so he would not have any future opportunity to wreck the director's parties. I don't know where he ended up. I never saw Charlie again.

Uh-Oh

THERE WAS ANOTHER UNFORGETTABLE patient who had been with Charlie in Ward F who never said a word. He usually had a smile on his face and his communication was mostly limited to an occasional grunt. I nicknamed him, "Uh-Oh," as every time he grunted, he would inevitably crap on himself. Obviously, poor Uh-Oh had chronic digestive problems and didn't poop like a normal person; it was more like cow patties in piles.

As I mentioned earlier, patients wore pants with no underwear and shoes with no socks, so frequently Uh-Oh would have poop running down his legs and filling up his shoes. When he walked, you could sometimes hear crap sloshing around in his shoes. There were at least two patients who followed Uh-Oh around with a mop and shovel to clean up after him all day long. These helpful patients were rewarded for their assistance with extra food and permission to stay up later at night. Sometimes Uh-Oh would just reach down in his pants with his hand to pull poop out, eating his own feces, and occasionally he would even come over smiling with crap between his teeth and dripping off his hand to offer you some. I always wondered if this is where the expression "shit-eating grin" came from.

I can hear Uh-Oh grunt now. Just the idea of it makes me think, "*Oh, shit!* Not again!"

LAST MONTH AT THE MADHOUSE

Like a Paid Vacation

I MANAGED TO ENDURE WORKING at the Callan Park Hospital for eight months. By then, I was contemplating quitting and had a plan to hit the road and explore Australia on my motorcycle. My plans to work at the hospital to save money for traveling had not worked out so well, but I was determined to follow my dream whether I had ample funds or not. I hadn't come all the way from America just to see some mental hospital wards and the beach now and then.

Ironically after all this time, now that I was thinking of leaving, the hospital finally decided to give me some much-needed training. The fact that they waited so late to train me was most likely due to the high turnover rate. Administration probably wanted to see if a new employee could handle the job before spending their time in training them.

About a month before I planned to quit, I got lucky and administration scheduled me for a one-week training class for nurses, both male and female. So far, I had been used primarily to help break up fights and had not had any real training as a nurse. Not only was the training class to be held in a clean, air-conditioned environment, but I would get to be with female staff members. After working so long in all-male wards (with few exceptions), this week of required training would be more like a paid vacation. When I heard about the training class, I strategically planned to wait to give my proper two-week notice upon completing the training course. Naturally, what guy wouldn't want to spend his time sitting down inside in a cool, air-conditioned room with attractive female employees versus being out in the hot courtyard in Ward F with Uh-Oh, or with Bart in Ward B?

Since I was leaving, I purposely didn't study for the final test and scored a whopping 58 out of 100! I'm sure the hospital thought (or at least I *hope* they thought) I turned in my notice due to my poor performance on the test. Little did they know my prior plans to quit! Thank you, Callan Park Hospital, for an amazing one-week vacation!

The first day when we broke for lunch, the group went to eat at a nearby hospital staff cafeteria. Man! I was unaware that a staff cafeteria even existed! Since each ward had its own kitchen and cafeteria, I always ate in the ward cafeteria with the patients or brown-bagged it. The staff cafeteria offered a better variety of food and most definitely a better environment than eating with mental patients.

The training class was made up of about 12 people and the hottest young, single female staff member was in the class! Wow! Did I get lucky! Mary had gorgeous, long black wavy hair and really pretty eyes. The class, a good mixture of guys and girls, sat together to eat lunch every day and everyone had fun talking and joking around. Another guy in the class ended up becoming my competitor for Mary's attention. The two of us had fun trading barbs at each other trying to impress this hot girl.

Although Mary was attractive and had a good personality, there seemed to be a certain sadness about her. I had the ability to make her laugh and I believe that's what she liked about me. This fun and games went on for the week of the training class and then Mary and I went our separate ways without setting up a date.

I turned in my two-week notice to the hospital. The first week of my two-week notice was spent working the graveyard shift from 6:30 p.m. to 6:30 a.m. for five nights straight, a total of 60 hours, followed by one week off. It turns out the fifth night of work was one of the worst nights of my entire employment there. I think, once again, the patients had not been given their meds and were acting out all night long. Consequently, I was unable to sneak into my secret locked room to get my usual night's sleep. It was an exhausting end to a grueling week!

I got home early in the morning and went straight to bed. Some time that afternoon, I was awakened by someone knocking on my door. I opened the door and was shocked to see that it was Mary! I had never told her where I lived, which added to the surprise of seeing her at my doorstep. She had obviously pulled some strings to get my address. I wondered if she had a friend who had access to the personnel files. There was a bulletin board on the hospital grounds that had employees' schedules posted, so she must have checked it to learn that I was off. Mary told me she had caught two different buses and finally a cab to bring her the rest of the way to my flat.

I finished getting dressed and we took a walk down Bondi Beach. She shared with me that she had had a fight with her live-in boyfriend, which explained some of the sadness that I had seen in her. We smoked a joint on the beach and smoked another joint back at my flat and enjoyed listening to music together. I realized she was simply using me, since I figured she would probably be going back to her boyfriend. At the same time, she knew that I was planning to hit the road to tour Australia the following week. The timing was not the best for either of us. However, neither of us minded taking advantage of our time alone, and the rest of the afternoon happened as you might imagine. Later that evening, I gave Mary a ride back to the hospital on my motorcycle so she could work her next shift. I never saw her again.

Draft Dodging

A FEW DOORS DOWN from my flat, I had become acquainted with a guy named Fred from New York. Fred was tall and skinny with curly hair and glasses and not particularly handsome. He told me that he was in Australia to avoid the draft. To avoid having to go fight in Vietnam, he told the military that he was a bed wetter. I wondered if this was even a legitimate reason for avoiding the draft. Personally, I would rather go to war than humiliate myself by claiming to wet the bed.

* * *

I, myself, wasn't worried about the draft. Due to my classification, I did not have to worry about being drafted. The military had me classified as 1-Y, which meant that I would only be drafted in the case of a declared war, such as World War III. My classification of 1-Y was due to a medical condition. When I was 18, I had to sign up for the draft and on my application was required to state any medical conditions that might affect my classification, so I filled in "asthma." I was also required to give the name of my physician. I figured if the military had any questions they would contact my doctor directly.

After receiving my draft card and seeing how the military had decided to classify me, I figured that they preferred to not risk enlisting anyone with a reoccurring medical condition. Obviously, they would not want me to have an asthma attack and have to air flight me back home for emergency medical attention.

As a child, on two different occasions, I almost died in the hospital. I had to be put in an oxygen tent to breathe, and I had to kick my legs just to get air into my lungs. Growing up, to help control the allergies that triggered my asthma attacks, I received desensitization shots three times a week. These shots were eventually tapered down to two times a week, then one until completed. Due to the allergy shots, going through puberty, and a rigorous body building workout in high school, my asthma was in remission. In fact, currently, I was in pretty darn good shape.

I never knew if the draft board checked with my doctor to confirm my 1-Y classification. At the time, the draft board had a lottery on television where they drew birthdates at random. The first 195 birthdates were called to serve in the order they were drawn. As I recall, my birthdate was in the high 200s and was never drawn to be drafted, so I would have never gone to Vietnam anyway.

All I know is, I was not in Australia to avoid the draft, but rather to do my wild hippie thing and tour the country. Becoming a hippie was tempting for me since I knew a lot of girls liked it. However, I was never against America, or our military, and have always strongly supported our troops overseas.

Preparing to Hit the Road

WHEN FRED LEARNED OF MY PLANS to quit the madhouse and tour the country, he decided to buy a motorcycle and join me. I didn't know Fred that well; in fact, I wasn't even sure I wanted any company. But Fred seemed excited about joining me, so with mixed emotions, I went along with the idea. At the time, touring the country together sounded like a great plan, but time would prove otherwise.

By this time, I had become skilled enough on my motorcycle to teach Fred how to ride his. I'm not sure where Fred's money came from. He didn't have to work like I did. While I had to sell my car in the states to buy my motorcycle, Fred's parents must have been funding his adventure in Australia, and just sent him money for a bike.

Before Fred and I hit the road, I arranged with Antonio, the guy who taught me how to ride my bike, to keep my extra belongings at his house while I was on the road. Before we departed, Fred and I decided to join the youth hostel organization. Hostels were located all over the country and provided a bunk bed and access to a kitchen and a bathroom as you traveled. They were usually large older homes where the men slept in one section and the women slept in another—supposedly.

* * *

When I joined the youth hostel organization, I paid a flat fee and received a membership card. As I traveled, I was required to sign in with my name and membership number in a guest book. Most hostels were managed by a married couple who did not live on the premises. The hostel manager would come by regularly to make sure guests were signed in appropriately and to ensure dishes were washed and beds were made. I usually got out of making my bed in the mornings by sleeping in my sleeping bag on top of the bed. Members were limited to a one-week stay—supposedly. The youth hostels turned out to be a great way to meet other young people who were traveling, especially Australian girls.

LIVING ON THE EDGE

Dirt Road to HELL!

I HEARD THROUGH FRIENDS that a good way for me and Fred to travel was to work as migrant workers picking fruit along the way. We were told we could probably find work in the town of Griffith, which is inland, southwest of Sydney. So, we set out on our bikes for Griffith. The farther inland we rode, the more we were getting into the real "Outback" that Australia is famous for. In fact, I saw my first wild kangaroos, two of them standing a little ways off the road watching us as we drove by. I got to see kangaroos a number of times during my stay in Australia, usually early in the mornings or late in the evenings.

Fred and I had a road map, but directions were not always clear due to inadequate road signs along the way. Sometimes we would stop and ask for directions, but it didn't take long to learn that it was a useless idea. With towns having Aboriginal names such as Wagga Wagga, Wallongong, Canowindra, Cootamundra, Wodonga, and Wongaratta, the people we asked might as well have been saying, "Ooh Eeh Ooh Ah Ah Ting Tang Walla Walla Bing Bang!" Needless to say, even after receiving detailed directions, frequently we were still confused as to where to go and how to get there.

On the way to Griffith, we stopped at a little roadside outpost and asked for directions. Since it was starting to rain, and nightfall was quickly approaching, we were told there was an abandoned house where we could take shelter. We had to take a red dirt road to get to the house and on the way, the rain started coming down even harder. We were riding street bikes, not dirt bikes, so we started having an issue with mud packing between the tire and the fender well. After some time, the mud was so heavily packed in that the tires would no longer turn. Fred and I found some sticks lying beside the road that we used to try to remove the mud from the tire fender wells. This helped, but only got us a little way before we had to stop to remove the mud again. After a while, we looked like drowned rats covered in red mud.

Darkness had fallen, the rain poured down fiercely, and thunder and lightning tore through the sky and lit up the night. Finally, Fred and I got the bright idea of riding *beside* the red dirt road out of the mud. But every few feet our front tires would drop into holes as large as gopher holes. In the bigger holes, the front of the motorcycle dropped so hard we were afraid it would break the front shocks on our bikes. We ended up having to get back onto the red dirt road. It was hours that we spent on this road to HELL.

Finally, we arrived at a crossroads. A pair of headlights cut through the dark as a car pulled up. The car was filled with four guys, and I guess they must have known we were lost, because they rolled down their window and the driver asked, "Where're you headed?"

"A few miles back, a fellow told us there was an abandoned house down this road where we could spend the night," I said. "Do you know where it is?"

"Man, I have no idea what house you're talking about, but you might as well get out of this hard rain and spend the night at our house. We're just a little way up this road from here."

"We hate to put you out," I said, thinking about how all the guys in the car looked a bit rough around the edges.

"Oh, no problem. Always room for two more!" the driver replied. "Come on. Follow us!"

Dirty, wet, and cold, it wasn't a difficult decision. We'd rather have a roof over our heads. Fred and I followed them down the muddy red dirt road. When we arrived, we saw eight to ten motorcycles parked in front of the house. We went in out of the rain into a room filled with young, rough-looking guys around our age doing their own thing. None of them seemed to take notice of our drenched, muddy appearance.

They were all wearing similar denim vests with the same logo. Apparently, we would be spending the night with some sort of motorcycle gang. All the guys were partying and drinking heavily. Despite their questionable character, Fred and I were just relieved to be changed out of our wet, muddy clothes and have a place to sleep out of the weather. We ended up sleeping on the floor on top of our sleeping bags. The drinking party carried on all night, but we were too exhausted to care.

* * *

About four o'clock in the morning, in the dark room, covered up with nothing more than a thin sheet, I felt something crawling on my foot. Major exhaustion had taken over from our earlier ordeal, and I was in such a deep sleep that I was only semi-aware as it continued to crawl up my leg under the sheet. When it reached my thigh, I looked up and saw the sheet move. I thought, "Hell, no!"'

I decided that whatever it was had crawled far enough. I threw the sheet back, knocked it off of me, and ran across the room to turn on the light to see what it was. I nearly puked when I saw a ginormous hairy spider almost the size of my hand running across the floor! The spider scurried over to the floorboard and, since it was an old house, there was plenty of room for him to crawl under through a crack and escape out of sight.

Anyone who knows me knows that I have an immense hatred for even little spiders, so there was no way I was going to lay back down on that floor to sleep. To play it safe, afraid the spider might come back out of hiding, or that it may have relatives in the house, I attempted to make a bed by pulling two dining room chairs together face to face. I sat in one chair, with my feet propped up in the other, and hoped I could rest until morning. But I didn't get any more sleep that night.

The next morning, Fred and I were eating a bowl of cereal for breakfast, as the same four guys that we met in the car the night before pulled up in the yard. They entered the house, each carrying cases of beer.

In total, there were ten or eleven guys hanging out at the house, along with a girl named Wendy, the girlfriend of a guy named Billy. Wendy was a pretty girl if you could overlook the large knife wound scar across her cheek.

Although it was only nine o'clock in the morning, since it had stopped raining, the whole gang went outside in the yard to continue their drinking. I wondered when they took time out to sleep. In an attempt to be sociable, Fred and I joined Billy and Wendy, who were separated from the rest of the gang on the opposite side of the yard. Those two seemed less intimidating than the ten guys who were chugging down beers.

Trying to think what to talk about, I said to Billy, "I like to hunt. Do you?"

Billy replied, "Oh yeah. Me and my buddies sometimes go wild pig hunting. In fact, if we don't see any wild pigs and get bored, we just hide behind trees and shoot at each other."

I BELIEVED HIM!

Just then, another car pulled up and two more guys got out with several more cases of beer. I mentioned to Billy and Wendy that I kept a small bag of marijuana hidden behind my headlight on my motorcycle. Wendy seemed to be particularly interested in smoking the pot, probably because she wasn't much of a beer drinker.

I went over to my motorcycle and loosened the four screws in the headlight with a Phillips screwdriver. Then I popped out the headlight to retrieve my small hidden bag of pot. The four of us sat down in the grass, Indian-style, while I rolled us a joint. While I was rolling the joint, one of the bikers from the other side of the yard staggered over. He must have weighed close to 300 pounds and was extremely drunk. He snatched the bag of pot from the ground and said, "What is *this* shit?" He then walked toward his buddies, clumsily spilling some of the pot out of the bag on the ground. This really pissed me off, but Fred and I weren't about to get into a fight with this many people to retrieve my pot, knowing we could spark a major fight with a motorcycle gang.

The next thing I knew, Wendy went running into the house and came back outside holding a rifle. I wondered, "What the crap! Is she going to start shooting?" Wendy turned the gun around backwards, so she was holding the barrel of the rifle in her hands and ran over toward the big 300-pound biker. He was showing the other bikers the bag and didn't see Wendy coming his way. She lunged forward and swung the rifle like a baseball bat, hitting him square in the face with the butt of the gun with all her might!

I'll never forget the sound the impact made. Blood spattered everywhere, and I'm sure she must have broken his nose. To my surprise, he didn't fall down; in fact, he threw a punch at Wendy, but missed. In a flash, Billy came running over, punching him in her defense. Then all hell broke loose! Man, I couldn't believe my eyes! This group of bikers, who seconds ago were drinking together like buddies, suddenly started fighting each other.

Meanwhile, Fred and I were still sitting Indian-style in the grass, taking this all in. My decision a few minutes earlier to remain calm in an attempt to maintain peace obviously failed. Eventually, they stopped throwing punches, and the whole group was staggering back and forth just holding onto each other.

"Man, he's bleedin' bad," one of them said, gesturing at the 300-pound biker, now lying semi-conscious in the grass. A few of the other bikers—fighting moments ago, but now friends again—hopped in the car to take him to the hospital.

Fred and I decided this was a good time to disappear.

We quickly went in the house and stuffed our clothes in our duffle bags. In the short time it took to pack up our stuff, a constable (Australia's term for the local sheriff), pulled up in the yard. I could hear the constable's conversation with Billy from inside the house.

The constable said, "Billy, I hear you've had trouble out here at the house again."

Billy replied, "Yes, sir."

The constable said, "Well, you know what happens if it happens again don't you?"

Billy replied, "Yes, sir." Then the constable slowly drove off.

I have no idea how the constable showed up so quickly at the house, unless he just happened to be cruising in the area and perhaps met up with the carload of drunks heading for the hospital. Fred and I just wanted to get out of there before the constable discovered what had started the brawl. Needless to say, we escaped while the getting was good.

Quickly making distance between us and the house and the red dirt road from hell, I thought about Wendy and how badly she must have wanted to smoke pot. The girl never even got one drag off my joint.

Moving On…

ORIGINALLY, FRED AND I had been headed north for the town of Griffith to find work. After all the confusion with directions, the ordeal of the red dirt road, and the craziness of the motorcycle gang, we ended up going southward toward Melbourne, which is located on the coast of Australia. The back roads took us across two rivers, the Murray River and the Murrumbidgee River. It was hot, and we were covered in red dust, so we decided to stop at a high metal bridge crossing one of these rivers in the middle of nowhere. It's been too long ago for me to remember which river, but I know it was a fairly wide one with a fast current, and we decided it would be a good place to jump in and cool off.

Fred and I parked our bikes and took off our shoes and shirts. I'm not really afraid of heights, but when we got out to the middle of the bridge and peered down at the water, we realized it was a lot farther down than we originally thought. After both of us hesitated a bit, I decided to jump first. Knowing if I tried diving head-first I'd probably break my neck, I took a deep breath, and jumped feet first. About halfway down, I realized I would be out of breath by the time I hit the water. Gasping for a second breath of air right before impact, I hoped for the best as I hit the water with a whopping, gigantic slash.

As soon as I came to the surface for air, Fred yelled down, "How was it?"

"Fine, come on in!" I lied. Fred jumped. When he came up to the surface, neither one of us proposed jumping a second time, nor did either one of us want to admit how truly scared we were. I am not sure if that high jump scared Fred as badly as it did me, but also like me, he wasn't about to admit it.

The swift current was taking us quickly downstream away from our bikes, so we swam for the bank. At that time, Fred and I were ignorant about the infamous crocodiles of Australia. I don't know if crocodiles were in these rivers this far south in 1971, but if they were, I feel like God was surely looking out for us. If we had kept jumping in and out of the water off the bridge, we surely would have attracted a hungry croc or two.

Since that day, I have imagined that a local Australian frequently driving by that bridge probably has a nice collection of abandoned motorcycles acquired from ignorant tourists like us.

Who's There?

As FRED AND I CONTINUED our journey toward Melbourne, we happened to stumble across work in the little town of Cobram. We would be working in an orchard picking apricots and thinning out peaches on peach trees for two weeks. We were instructed to whack clusters of peaches with a long stick to thin them out, enabling the remaining peaches to grow larger. Fred and I joined a work crew of five other hippie employees: two hippie couples and one tall guy that we simply called "Riverman" because he mostly lived on the Murray River by himself.

The sleeping quarters was a concrete block building consisting of individual beds in each room. The concrete walls dividing the rooms did not go all the way to the ceiling, so you could easily hear what was going on in the adjacent rooms. The first night, sleeping in these minimal accommodations, is when I first learned Fred was kind of weird. About four o'clock in the morning, I hear Fred saying in a loud voice, "Who's there?" Then again, I hear, "Who's there? Who's THERE? WHO'S THERE!?" Then came a blood-curdling holler that sounded like someone being murdered!

By now I'm wide awake, my eyes as large as saucers! I'm wondering, "Am I next? Is someone going room to room killing people with an axe?" The light came on in Fred's room and I figured it was just a bad nightmare. But maybe it was the axe murderer who turned on the light? I didn't sleep well the rest of the night.

The rest of the two weeks went by rather uneventfully other than multiple encounters with bees as I traveled on my motorcycle. I didn't have a face shield on my helmet (a bad idea), so frequently bees would get wedged between my helmet and my head and sometimes get tangled in my hair. Angry at being trapped, the bees buzzed loudly as they tried to escape. Each time, before I could prevent getting stung, I would have to quickly down shift through each of my motorcycle's five gears, pull off the road, put the kick stand down, and yank my helmet off, --but it was always too late. One time I was stung on top of the head, another time on my temple, and another time on the ear.

The last time, I had a shirt and jacket on and the bee flew down the back of my neck, under my collar, and into my shirt. Again, I had to quickly down shift through all five gears, pull off the road, put the kick stand down, yank off my jacket, and unbutton my shirt, but once again, --I was too late. Over the years, I've occasionally wondered if a passing car with a farmer and his wife might have noticed me frantically stripping off my clothes beside the road and commented to his wife, "Look, honey, another drug-crazed hippie!"

Thankfully, Fred and I got along well with the other hippie employees on the farm and we enjoyed eating and hanging out together. The group of us smoked up what little pot I had left and told me they would replace what we had smoked. It turned out that one of the guys knew where three eight-foot-tall marijuana plants were. I have a photograph, to this day, of the whole group posing with a garbage bag full of pot. Hoping to not incriminate myself, I volunteered to be the photographer of the group and stay out of the picture. The sad part of the story is that the pot had not been cured yet, so it turned out to be of no benefit to me or Fred before we had to hit the road again.

THREE WEEKS AT THE MELBOURNE HOSTEL

Extended Stay

CONTINUING SOUTHWEST, we stayed at one of the first and oldest hostels in the country. It was a big old house with a rain barrel that provided water for the guests. One evening, I was taking a drink out of a glass and looked down to see something small in the water with eyeballs looking back at me. It turned out to be mosquito larvae. High protein H_2O!

As I previously stated, we were only supposed to stay one week at a time at any youth hostel. Since Fred and I got a three-week job picking weeds on a tulip farm, we needed to stay at the Melbourne hostel for a full three-week period. Fortunately, the caretakers were slack on keeping up with the guest registry and did not notice our extended stay.

Our pay for pulling weeds on the tulip farm was a whopping one dollar an hour! The physical work may not have been so miserable if the tulips had been in bloom. However, we were basically just pulling weeds out of red dirt hills for eight hours a day in 100-degree heat. Definitely, this job taught me the value of a dollar!

Week One

DESPITE THE EXHAUSTING WORK, the Melbourne hostel turned out to be a gold mine for meeting Australian girls who were on vacation backpacking and hitchhiking. The first week I meet Debbie, who had hitchhiked alone from Sydney to Melbourne. She worked at a hospital in Sydney as the phlebotomist, or more simply stated, the nurse who drew blood.

Debbie was a short brunette with a nice figure. We got to know each other during evening meals after I got off work on the tulip farm. Debbie and I had some fun rides on my motorcycle and we enjoyed visiting some of the nearby parks together.

As I said before, the hostels were divided up with females on one side and males on another side. As luck would have it, Debbie ended up having the female side of the hostel all to herself. Being the gentlemen that I am, and not wanting Debbie to be lonely, I decided to join her on the women's side for the night. I don't claim to be God's gift to women, but she was the most vocal woman I have ever had sex with. I was trying to be discreet, but *my*, she was hollering like an alley cat! Then, after all this hollering, there was a long pause of silence. I lay there wondering if I had somehow killed her. Finally, she said, "That was beautiful!" A comment to boost to any man's ego!

* * *

Debbie stayed at the hostel for three or four days before heading back to Sydney. I told her I would still be at the hostel for about two more weeks. After she returned to Sydney, I was surprised to receive an eight-page letter from Debbie. I guess she was hoping for a long-term relationship, but I knew I had not planned to get serious with anyone during this time in my life. Since this happened so long ago now, I can't remember if I even responded to her letter, but, needless to say, I haven't forgotten her screams.

Week Two

A FEW DAYS AFTER DEBBIE left, Barbara showed up at the hostel. Like Debbie, she also had been backpacking and hitchhiking. Barbara was a classic surfer girl from head to toe. She had long, straight blonde hair, beautiful perfect white teeth, tan lines, and a 38D bust. She had a good figure, but was a big built girl, with a large frame. Guys today might use the term "thick." But Barbara was "thick" in all the right places.

It was common to get acquainted with other hostel members in the kitchen, or in the dining area while eating a meal together. One day while Barbara was eating lunch with me, she mentioned that she would like to go to the beach. This was, of course, long before GPS or internet. Although we had a map, we were clueless as to how long it would take to get there. On the spur of the moment, we decided to put on our swimsuits under our jeans and shirts, grab some towels, and head off for the beach.

* * *

As we rode together on my motorcycle, the weather quickly turned bad on us. It started raining and getting colder as we got into later afternoon and it was taking much longer to get to the beach than we expected. Finally, we arrived, both soaked through. Barbara took her shirt and jeans off to take a swim. I didn't go swimming and Barbara just swam for a short while before getting out. I'm not sure exactly why I didn't swim, too, other than being too cold and too stupid. The water was probably warmer than the air and I probably missed out on a romantic swim with Barbara. It's been a long time, but I still remember her in that black bikini with her long blonde hair blowing in the breeze.

We hit the road again to head back to the hostel, but the weather got worse, and colder. The frigid rain beat down on us and lightening flashed in the darkened sky. My yellow-tinted glasses fogged up, making it difficult to see, and without a shield on our helmets, the rain was stinging our faces. For sure, we didn't want to take the long drive back and decided to get a place to stay overnight.

Eventually we came across a campground, and I pulled in to check if we could rent a camper trailer. Thankfully, they had a vacancy, as well as a laundromat where we could dry our clothes.

The camper we rented had both a full-size and a single bed in it. The lady who rented us the camper gave us clean linens for both beds. Also, they had a public shower facility where we could take warm showers one person at a time. I let Barbara shower first and then I took my turn. When I got back to the camper, to my surprise, Barbara had already made up the full-size bed and threw back the covers to show me she was naked in the bed and welcomed me with a big smile on her face. I know you probably won't believe me when I say this, but I *was* caught by surprise. I sincerely had no expectations beforehand, but I was willing to go with the flow.

It could have rained and poured and stormed that night, but, as you would imagine, we had no clue about the weather outside—we were preoccupied with more important things. The next morning, I woke up to Barbara shaking me with that same tempting, mischievous smile on her face. Well, you know me—I just go with the flow.

Not long after we returned to the hostel in Melbourne, Barbara had to pack up her things to hitchhike back home. I do not remember where her home was, and I had no further contact with her. *Such was the hippie life...*

Week Three

MY THIRD WEEK at the Melbourne hostel, I met a cute girl named Candy who lived in Toowong, near Brisbane. Brisbane is the capital city of the state of Queensland and, being in the tropical part of the country, is considered the "sunshine" state of Australia. Candy had long, dark brown wavy hair, a Marilyn Monroe beauty mark on her face, a nice tan, and long legs that appeared to go up to her neck. Candy was a college student who shared a house with two other girls and a guy named Bob. Bob, I later found out, had a thing for her and wanted to be more than her friend.

She was traveling with Sue, one of her female roommates. Candy and I hit it off right away, but it was kind of awkward because Sue wasn't that attracted to my traveling companion, Fred. It ended up that for a couple days, Candy and I had to do our own thing and just let Sue and Fred fend for themselves.

* * *

Candy and Sue were heading out on the road again that weekend for a three-day outdoor concert near the Murray River, located north of Melbourne. The concert featured Stephen Stills of Crosby, Stills and Nash fame and other local talent. Before Candy left, she encouraged me and Fred to join them, but we were still working on the tulip farm during the day and had to finish our work week out through Friday. When we knocked off work, we headed out to meet up with Candy and Sue at the Murray River.

En route to the concert, I noticed a large white bird about the size of a seagull, flying slowly across the pasture to my left. I didn't pay it any mind until it collided with me, hitting me hard in the Adam's apple. The bird flipped and rolled in mid-air and proceeded to slowly fly away as if nothing had happened. But I had to fight the tears as I down shifted five gears on my bike so I could pull over to the side of the road. This turned out to be just one more of the many flying objects that I encountered on my travels.

As we approached the concert, traffic was backed up at the entrance. Some people in a pickup truck noticed me and Fred on our motorcycles waiting in the long line. They told us they were returning to the concert after picking up supplies in town and said, "Park your motorcycles and we will hide you under a tarp with our supplies in the back of our truck."

They told us that once we entered, if we had to leave, security at the entrance would stamp our hand so we could return. So, we slipped in to the venue underneath their tarp, turned right around to exit, got our hands stamped, and then retrieved our motorcycles to go back in. What a break!

* * *

People were allowed to park vehicles at their camping sites along the river, so Fred and I drove down a winding dirt road through the campgrounds and the crowds. Amazingly, we spotted Candy and Sue waving at us from a distance. It was sort of a miracle that they spotted us among so many people!

The girls directed us to their campsite, which was a lean-to built out of cut tree limbs. Candy failed to tell me that her other two roommates, Bob and Kathy, had also planned to join them at the concert. Bob had gone to great lengths to build a nice shelter for the three days they planned to be there. The lean-to seemed rather small for all four of the roommates. I couldn't help but wonder if perhaps Bob had built it more specifically for him and Candy, whom I knew he was trying to impress. I can't recall what happened to Bob, Fred, Sue, or Kathy at the concert, but I do remember that the lean-to became my and Candy's little "love shack" for a couple days. Surely, Bob hates me to this very day, but I honestly did not plan for things to turn out that way.

One hot afternoon, while we were trying to cool off in the Murray River, I decided to swim across to the other side, but the river was pretty wide and the current stronger than it looked. About halfway across, I was getting really tired of fighting the current and had my doubts that I would make it across. Fortunately, I spotted a large boulder close by, just below the water's surface, and swam for it. I climbed up on top of the boulder to take a break only to realize I was attracting a lot of attention from spectators. People were laughing and pointing at me because it appeared as if I was actually walking on water. I knew Jesus walked on water, but at this time in my life, I knew the only thing I had in common with Jesus was my long hair.

When the concert was over, Candy and I discussed meeting up again in Tasmania, but she and Sue had other commitments. Fred and I drove on our motorcycles from the concert south to Melbourne. We heard we could find work in Tasmania picking apples. Once again, the plan was to work a while and then travel to see the sights.

TASMANIA

Beggars Can't Be Choosy

THE ONLY WAY from the mainland of Melbourne to the island of Tasmania was by ferry boat. Fred and I drove to the port in Melbourne and boarded the ferry with our motorcycles. The ferry ride took all night to get to Tasmania. Unlike a ship, there were no beds, simply hard benches to sit on, and the crossing was a long, uncomfortable trip. Finally, at daybreak, we were relieved to be approaching the port. The fog was burning off, revealing a majestic panoramic view of the huge rocky shoreline. I had heard of how beautiful Tasmania was with its mountainous terrain covered in different shades of green. Now I was getting excited to see the island for myself.

Shortly after we arrived, we left the port and began looking for a gas station to fill up. Reality hit hard when we discovered that after paying for gas and the ferry boat ride, we were basically broke. Nothing like being 10,000 miles from home on an island, knowing no one, and realizing you're out of money. Fred and I pulled off to the side of the road to discuss our grim situation.

After a lengthy conversation, needing to chill out and momentarily escape our challenging circumstances, I decided to pull out my little portable radio from my duffle bag tied across the back of my bike. As soon as I turned it on, we heard the lyrics to the song, "Like a Rolling Stone" by Bob Dylan. The words came out loud and clear. We burst out laughing. In fact, I laughed so hard, I cried!

Darkness was approaching, so Fred and I decided to sleep in the woods in our sleeping bags and then search for a job the next morning. There was a chill in the night air and I zipped my mummy sleeping bag up all the way to my neck. Yes, it was cold in the woods that night, but I was comfortable in my sleeping bag.

About two o'clock in the morning, sound asleep, I suddenly heard Fred holler loud and clear, "DON'T MOVE! DON'T MOVE!"

My eyes popped wide open and I wondered if a snake or some wild animal was ready to attack me. Straining my eyes to see in the dark, I looked all around me but did not see anything threatening. Warm and cozy, I definitely wasn't planning on moving if I didn't have to. I went back to sleep realizing it was simply Fred having another one of his weird dreams and talking in his sleep.

The next morning, we checked with several different apple farms for jobs. In the town of Huon at Castle Forbes Bay, we found an apple farmer who would hire us to pick apples. The only problem was, the apples would not be ready to pick for another week. Thankfully, the farmer told us we could go ahead and stay in one of the migrant shacks until the apples were ready.

I don't really remember the bedding situation other than that we slept on top of a mattress in our sleeping bags. Quite vivid in my mind, however, was the unique round wooden bathtub. To heat the water for a bath, each morning, we had to fill the tub, plug in an electrical cord, and the water would be warm when we returned in the evening. That meant only one person could take a bath each night, unless you were willing to share someone's dirty bath water. Not willing to take that route, Fred and I agreed to take turns, alternating nights to bathe.

The farmer gave us a tour of the apple orchard. We followed behind him as we walked past rows of apple trees loaded with beautiful, mature, green Granny Smith apples. The acres of trees were in neat, orderly rows and, obviously, well maintained. As we walked along, he warned, "Any snake that you see in Australia is poisonous." No sooner had he said it that a skinny, lime-green snake about six feet long slithered near us through the grass really fast! That gave me and Fred a moment to pause and ponder—and to reconsider our job opportunity. It wasn't really a good thought, being high up a ladder in an apple tree with green leaves and suddenly trying to escape a fast, camouflaged green deadly snake without falling.

As the farmer continued his tour of the property, he said, "I think it is funny that little old ladies in Tasmania have native opium plants growing wild in their flower gardens." I put this bit of information in my memory bank for future reference.

Now, I had to consider if it would be best to die quickly from a poisonous snake bite or suffer a slow death from starvation. Not willing to go hungry, we reluctantly agreed to work at the apple orchard.

We had a place to stay for a week before we started to work, but we still had the difficult situation of having no money and no food. Obviously, we were surrounded by apple trees loaded with apples, so Fred and I ate a lot of raw apples. For the following two weeks until our first payday, we figured we could survive on apples. We found some basic staples left in our shack from previous migrant workers. Sometimes for variety, we sliced up our raw apples and added salt and pepper. Desperate to change it up, we even took time to stew apples on the gas stove. It's a wonder, to this day, that I can even look at an apple, let alone eat one.

Later, during the same week, we discovered there were potatoes planted between the rows of apple trees. This was indeed a gold mine to us! Boiled potatoes were a nice change from eating nothing but apples, day after day. In addition to salt and pepper, we managed to find butter left behind in the shack's refrigerator to put on our potatoes! The farmer's wife must have felt sorry for us as she brought us raw milk, warm and fresh from their cow. After chilling in the refrigerator, the cream would strangely gather on top, a characteristic of unpasteurized milk that we weren't familiar with, but we were sure thankful to have it! It's not fun to be scrounging and foraging for something to eat. After going through this food crisis in my life, I developed a great appreciation for a good home-cooked meal.

A Night to Remember

IN ADDITION TO HAVING TO BE CREATIVE at meal time, we were dying of sheer boredom from not working and were tired of having no money to go anywhere. It seemed like the longest week in history waiting for the farmer to say the apples were ready to pick.

Finally, we got to go to work, but we were then anxious for our first payday, having long ago had our fill of apples and potatoes. Thankfully, once we got busy picking apples every day, time seemed to pass much faster. Before we knew it, we had completed a week of work and after getting paid that Friday, the money was burning a hole in our pockets.

* * *

That evening, back at the shack, we got cleaned up, and since we were out in the country, far from anywhere to go out to eat, we were forced to eat once again from our limited menu of apples and potatoes, hoping it would be the last such meal for a while. Bored, with nothing to do for entertainment, about ten o'clock that night, Fred and I got a great idea.

We knew Candy and Sue were going to be staying at a hostel on the northern part of the island, so we hurriedly packed some of our clothes in our duffle bags and headed in their direction. We knew the girls were located on the coastline, but we really had no idea of how long it would take to get there, or what kind of weather we might run into along the way.

As we traveled toward the hostel, hoping to meet up with the girls, the weather got colder, and it started raining. The road was desolate and deserted. Nothing but endless dark woods flanked both sides of the paved road, with the only light being the headlights on our motorcycles.

At some point, I heard something growling and running out of the woods from the right side of the road and it hit the front wheel of my motorcycle, almost knocking me down. I thought, "What was THAT!? That was freaking scary!" Then in a matter of a few seconds, out of the pitch-black darkness, I got hit in the front wheel again and I had to extend my left foot to catch my balance on the wet pavement. Fred and I sped up hoping to escape whatever was trying to attack us, but I still managed to get hit on the front wheel two more times.

When Fred and I arrived at the next little town, I motioned for Fred to pull over to discuss what happened back there in the dark.

"What the hell was that back there?" I said.

Fred, all hyped up, responded, "I don't know, but I got hit three times!"

"I got hit four times!" I said. "I'm sure glad we didn't wreck, because whatever it was meant business and was surely planning to eat us alive!"

With further conversation, we concluded that it must have been a pack of dingoes spread throughout the dark woods. Dingoes are roaming wild dogs, native to Australia, that are major predators and a threat to livestock and wildlife. I was just glad that we didn't end up on their menu that night.

This trip to see the girls had now turned into a miserable four-hour ordeal driving in and out of cold, drenching rain. Finally, we saw a city limit sign and were happy to know we were near our destination. I was leading as we approached a steep descending hill traveling about 60 miles per hour. Suddenly I was bouncing from one leg to the other struggling to keep my bike upright! After frantically somehow managing to not wipe out, I turned my head back toward Fred and yelled, "WHAT A SAVE!"

As the old saying goes, "Pride comes before the fall..." Immediately, I flew off my bike and crashed down onto the asphalt on my left side. The bike and I went sliding side by side down the steep paved highway. Sparks from my crash bars were flying everywhere, like Fourth of July fireworks! Then, after sliding for what seemed like the length of a football field, the bike and I came to a stop.

Lying there in shock for a few seconds, I attempted to catch my breath. It is fortunate that I had on a helmet, as I knew the left side of my head and body took the brunt of the impact. I knew I needed to try to stand up to evaluate the damage to both myself and my bike. The yellow tinted prescription glasses that I wore for nighttime driving were crushed, leaving a gash over my right eyebrow. Like most head wounds, it was bleeding profusely. My left hand was throbbing and I wondered if it was broken.

I noticed that Fred had managed to safely drive off to the side of the road and had parked his bike. Since it was before daylight, there was no traffic to deal with. As Fred stepped back into the highway, the road was so slippery, he literally had to crawl on all fours to come to my aid. Once we managed to get me and the bike out of the road, we tried to assess the damage to the bike. The metal crash bars were halfway eaten through but had done their job and protected the engine. My left blinker light was broken, but, thankfully, the bike had suffered no major damage.

Accessing our surroundings, we realized that the bottom of the hill where I had managed to slide to a stop just happened to be at an intersection. Across from the intersection was a park, and, again, as I mentioned earlier, it was good there was no traffic. I slowly and painfully pushed my bike a short distance across the road and retreated to a picnic table to recuperate and figure out what to do next. We discussed my accident in detail and concluded that large trucks had been dropping oil on the highway and the rain had made the surface slick with the oil.

Fred and I decided the gash over my right eyebrow probably needed stitches, so our plan was for me to lie back on the picnic table, putting pressure on the gash to help stop the bleeding while Fred went to find the nearest hospital. As I lay on the table, I could feel the cold of the night and the dampness of the wooden boards below me creeping in. I was aching pretty bad, and my left hand was starting to swell. At least the rain had stopped.

Shortly, I heard a car approaching on the highway. As it came nearer, it slowed down, and I grew a bit concerned when it turned into the park, but I was now in so much throbbing pain that I didn't really care.

As the car circled inside the park, it illuminated me and the picnic table in its bright white headlights. As I squinted my eyes, I could now distinguish the outline of a cop car.

I continued to lay on the table unconcerned as the constable got out of the car and approached me. He said, "I see you pranged your motorcycle." (As you probably figured, "pranged" is an Australian word for wrecked or crashed.) The constable nearly knocked me over with the smell of alcohol on his breath. "You haven't been drinking, have you?" he said *to me*.

I replied, "No, I haven't been drinking. The wreck was caused by the oil on the wet pavement coming into town. My buddy Fred went to look for a hospital so I can get stitches over my eye."

"Boy, there's no hospital in this town. The nearest hospital is through those mountains," the constable interjected as he pointed far off in the distance.

Awkward, in my reclined position, I attempted to strain my neck to look in the direction he was pointing. Barely visible through the fog, I could make out a distant mountain ridge.

"Can you take me to the hospital?"

"No."

Not exactly the answer I expected from an officer.

"I am in no shape to drive those mountains tonight," he said.

Thankfully, this drunken officer had enough wits about him to know his limitations!

I explained the reason we arrived in his town was that we were looking for the hostel. Just then, Fred drove up on his motorcycle. The constable offered to lead us there. We drove a short distance to the hostel and made our grand entrance through the front door. I figured he would leave after leading us there, but I wonder if perhaps the influence of alcohol had clouded his judgment. Nothing like arriving at 2:30 in the morning while everyone in the hostel is sound asleep with a constable shining his bright flashlight in people's faces as he tried to help us locate Candy and Sue! Maybe he wanted to check the girls out for himself?

The house was packed with guys and girls sleeping all around on the floor in sleeping bags since all the bunk beds were taken. Finally, we located Candy and Sue, so the constable left. The girls were some of the fortunate ones who got bunk beds. So, I climbed in the top bunk with Candy for some TLC after a rough night and Fred crawled in with Sue on the lower bunk.

The next morning, Fred and Candy convinced me that I needed to go to the hospital to get an x-ray on my left hand to make sure it wasn't broken and to see if I needed stitches over my right eye. Candy offered to ride with me, but I wasn't confident to carry another person on the back of my motorcycle in my condition. Consequently, I drove there on my own. The x-ray showed that my hand wasn't broken, and the cut over my eye had already closed and, amazingly, healed to the point that no stitches were necessary. But I am pretty sure to this day that I am carrying some Tasmanian road tar in the scar over my eye.

Where There's a Will, There's a Way

WHEN I LEFT THE HOSPITAL, I decided to pick up a fruit and cheese basket and a bottle of wine with the idea of a romantic night on the beach with Candy. The beach was in walking distance of the hostel where we were staying. That night was dimly lit: no moon, only stars to light our way to the beach as Candy and I walked over sand dunes covered with sea oats. We were carrying a beach blanket, our basket and a bottle of wine, and, needless to say, I was carrying great expectations.

Candy was walking a short distance in front of me when I heard the loud, awful sound, "AWKKK!" Instantly, Candy screamed, turned around, and ran smack into me as she attempted to escape whatever it was. I was trying to focus my eyes to see what had scared her, only to see not one, but over a hundred penguins running toward the water! In the dark Candy had accidentally stepped on one of the penguins, causing it to send out an alarm to his colony of friends. It was really funny to see all of them waddling from side to side as they ran for the ocean.

During the day, you could see a small island in the distance covered with penguins, but we had no idea that they came to the mainland during the night. It didn't take long to discover that the beach was littered with penguin poop, ruining my romantic plans. How many people can say they had a romantic evening on the beach ruined by a penguin?

That night, we had to go to Plan B. We ended up at a picnic table at a park not far from the beach and made the best of the situation—no blanket needed.

TASMANIA

The Scientific Method

THE TIME CAME FOR CANDY and Sue to start hitchhiking back to Queensland and for Fred and I to go back to the farm to pick apples. I told Candy that when I got back to the mainland, I would meet up with her again in Queensland. Fred and I worked for about three more weeks picking apples and almost got fired because Fred was so slow at picking. While I was working, I started thinking about what the farmer said about opium plants growing wild in Tasmania. Since I had run out of pot, I thought to myself, "I would really like to have something to smoke." The only problem was, I didn't know what an opium plant looked like.

Of course, during the '70s there was no Google or internet to make it easy to research opium, so I went to a library to look it up. First chance I got, on one of my days off, I went to the nearest town with a library, cracked open an encyclopedia, and turned to the "O" section. But when I got to the page that was supposed to have a picture of the plant, I saw the page was torn out. Hmm, I thought to myself, I must be on to something.

I chose another encyclopedia, and this time managed to find an actual picture of an opium plant. Aha! I'd seen that plant growing near the steps beside the farmer's house!

The book showed a very recognizable plant with a long stem and a large round seed pod about the size of a tomato on top. I learned that the seed pods, which form under a variety of different colored flowers, is surprisingly classified as a fruit. The text explained that the traditional way to extract the opium is from a seed pod that is still green, not after it is dead and dried up. The book stated, "When green, incisions are made on the seed pods and a latex substance oozes from incisions and is collected once dried."

Well, the plant that I remembered seeing at the farmer's house had no flower on top and the seed pod, due to a killing frost, was brown, not green. But, desperate to replace my pot, I decided to go to the farmer's house to swipe one of his wife's two opium pods beside their front porch, hoping to make it not so obvious that one was missing. I took the stolen brown pod back to the shack, crushed it, and rolled it up with a paper like a joint.

That night I went in my room and sat on my bed to smoke my new opium joint, but after a few minutes wasn't feeling like it had any affect. Walking down the long hallway toward Fred's bedroom, I said, "Fred, I don't think this opium is working." As I spoke the words, I suddenly felt myself bouncing from one wall to the other. I managed to get myself to the entrance of his bedroom.

Fred, observing that I wasn't doing so well said, "Man, let's go outside! You need some fresh air!" He followed me as I staggered out of the shack, unaware that a severe headache and stomach cramps were soon to follow. I took several deep breaths of the cool night air.

Fred said, "I don't think I want to try it after *your* ordeal," and left me to go back inside.

I stayed outside, pacing back and forth for about thirty minutes before my symptoms subsided. My DIY opium attempt turned out *not* to be the "fun" experience I anticipated. I said to myself, "I will never try that again!"

Making Plans

FORTUNATELY, FOLLOWING THE WARNING from the farmer about all the deadly snakes in Tasmania, since the first day on the farm, Fred and I never saw another snake. Also, *fortunately*, if the farmer's wife had happened to notice the missing opium plant, she never said anything.

* * *

Around this time, I received a letter from my brother Mike telling be about the pain he was going through in dealing with a divorce. I was blown away when I read that he had found God and said that he would share more details with me when I arrived home. I wrote him back:

Mike,

> *I was really moved and surprised by your letter. I was hoping things would work out for you because of all the hard times you have had. The part about God in your letter surprised me, as it would you if you received a letter like that from me. We will have to talk about it when I get home.*
> --Pat

During these last three weeks of working in Tasmania, I was thinking of returning home to America. The letter from Mike had got me thinking of home and made me realize that I *was* actually a little homesick. I was missing family and the change of seasons in Georgia. I especially missed the beautiful fall time of year with the green leaves changing to vibrant reds, oranges, and yellows. In the United States, the winter months of November, December, January, and February are Australia's summer months. But due to my love for the beach, I was thinking that when I returned home, it would be cool to have two summers in one year. Currently, during March and April, I was experiencing Australia's fall months and knew that if I returned to the U.S. during the next month, in May, I would arrive just in time for June, July, and August.

Originally, before leaving for Australia, I had considered staying there permanently. But with the cost of living being so high and it being so hard to get ahead for the middle class, especially with the unions going on strike so often, I had second thoughts. As you know, I thought I would be escaping the political and social unrest of America, but I concluded from my stay in Australia that all countries have their issues.

My thought process led me to the decision to go home, so I decided to return to the mainland en route back to Sydney.

I discussed my new plans with Fred. He decided to stay in Tasmania to earn extra money. Of course, I knew he couldn't go home yet, since he was avoiding the draft. Parting ways with Fred was not a disappointment as it seemed that I had to "mother" him all over Australia. By that, I mean I always had to take the lead and plan where we went. I was always the one who had to do the talking when we applied for a job, and Fred was the one who would almost get us fired for not being a good worker. And of course, he talked out loud in his sleep and was a third wheel with the girls. I lacked respect for a draft dodger, not to mention that he helped to smoke up my dope and never offered to replace it. I gladly took off for Sydney and never saw Fred again.

BACK TO THE MAINLAND

Kick-A-Rock Trick

AFTER FRED AND I PARTED WAYS, I took a ferry boat from the island of Tasmania back to Melbourne on the mainland. From there, I was heading back to Sydney to make final arrangements before returning to America. I needed to retrieve my possessions that I left at Antonio's and sell my motorcycle so I could afford a ticket home on an ocean liner.

Riding on my motorcycle from the coast of Melbourne to the city of Sydney was a long and boring trip. To entertain myself, I invented a game—perhaps better described as a bad habit—of randomly kicking rocks on the paved roadway with my foot.

Unfortunately, one of the times I did my little kick-a-rock trick, the rock did not move. With excruciating pain, my eyes filled with tears and immediately I pulled off to the side of the road. I felt like I had broken all the toes in my foot! I limped over to check out the so-called "rock" and realized it was permanently attached to a five-foot solid rock slab. If I had been wearing steel-toed boots, I might not have been suffering so, but I was just wearing tennis shoes. Lesson learned. No more rock kicking!

* * *

When I arrived back in Sydney, I first went to visit Antonio. He had been good enough to keep my possessions during my road trip and now he offered to let me stay at his house for a few days. During this time, I sold my motorcycle and used the money to book an ocean liner back to America. The earliest departure date was about a week and half away. I thought, "What better way to spend my last week in the country than with Candy!"

I called Candy to tell her that I wanted to take a train north to Brisbane to see her. Candy said with no hesitation, "Great! I'll pick you up at the train station."

When I arrived in the city of Brisbane, Candy met me as planned and drove me to her house in the suburb of Toowong, where she shared a house with Sue, along with another girl, and Bob, a med student who I had met at the outdoor concert on the Murray River. Yes, the same "Bob," the Bob who built a lean-to just for himself and Candy and which I *innocently* took over. I knew Bob had a thing for her and now I was moving into a house with him and Candy for a week. If Bob didn't hate me before, he surely would now.

BACK TO THE MAINLAND

It's Worse Than We Thought!

CANDY AND HER ROOMMATES were all full-time students at the local university and were all working part-time jobs. Candy attended classes during the day and worked part-time as a waitress at a pub, so most of the day I was alone at the house. Strangely, I cannot remember the name of the university, whether it was in the suburb of Toowong or Brisbane, or what Candy's major was, but there are some things you just don't forget.

* * *

They had a huge chalkboard in the living room that Candy and her roommates used to write messages on. One day, sitting in the house, bored and smoking a joint, I decided to be creative. I wrote on the chalkboard in big letters and little letters, vertically, horizontally, and diagonally, repetitively, the following words, "SEX IS FUN!!!" I had just sat down and was admiring my handiwork when I heard a knock on the front door. Answering the door, I was shocked to see a Catholic priest standing there, dressed in traditional attire with the white collar.

"Hello. I'm here to see Candy," the priest said.

"She's not home yet from the university," I replied.

Looking at his watch, he responded, "She gets out of class at about three o'clock. So, she'll be home shortly." Then he added, "Do you mind if I come in and wait for her?"

Temporarily forgetting about my fine artwork boldly displayed in the living room, I invited him in. The priest sat down on the couch directly facing the chalkboard. I knew Catholics drink alcohol, but I didn't know if it was socially acceptable to offer a priest a beer or a joint.

"Uh, would you like a drink of water?" I said.

Attempting to make small talk with him felt like an eternity before Candy showed up. She walked in and gave the priest a hug and immediately invited him to move from the living room into the dining room to talk. Obviously, she saw the "elephant in the room," but was ignoring it for now. To give them some privacy, I left and went to the bedroom. The two of them talked for about an hour and as soon as the priest left, Candy came into the bedroom and slugged me in the shoulder.

"What were you thinking?" she asked.

"Obviously, I was thinking sex was fun!"

Yes, I felt like a scolded dog at this point. In my defense, I explained that I was bored, staying alone all day, and had no clue a Catholic priest would be coming to the house.

It turned out that Candy's mom, a devout Catholic, sent the priest to visit and invite Candy to come back to church and get on the right path. No doubt, the priest had not only read my artwork on the bulletin board, but had also noticed the lingering smell of pot in the air. I wondered if he reported back to her mom, "It's worse than we thought!" Thankfully, it wasn't long before Candy forgave me and things were back to normal between us.

Tripping Grass

ON A FRIDAY NIGHT, everyone in the house had made plans to go to the movies together. Before we left, a guy I had not seen before showed up. I don't remember his name, but I remember Candy pulling me aside and telling me that he had once robbed a bank. This guy mentioned that he had some tripping grass. Tripping grass is marijuana that is laced with a hallucinatory drug. The guy kept going on and on about his tripping grass, so the five of us decided to smoke one of his joints before leaving the house for the movies. Although all of us were sharing the one joint, it was so powerful that we quit after smoking it only halfway down.

By the time we got to the movie theater, I was seeing different colors, my ears were ringing, and all the sounds and people talking in the movie were unrecognizable or simply "noise." For me, the movie was a total waste of both money and time, because I wasn't able to comprehend anything.

The next night at the house, for some reason, the five of us decided to smoke the other half of our joint left over from the night before. Although I had experienced the weird side effects at the theater, and wondering if it was just me, I tried it again. This time, Candy fell onto the floor and went into convulsions. This freaked everyone out, but her severe, violent reaction also managed to quickly sober everyone up. The doctor among us, Bob, had us get her on her feet and keep her awake.

Later, as the effects wore off, Candy said she was willing to try it again.

"Are you freaking crazy?" I asked her.

We ended up having an argument over smoking the junk. When I smoked regular pot, it relaxed me and was enjoyable. This stuff was not enjoyable and it sure was not normal to have convulsions from smoking pot.

The incident with the opium plant back in Tasmania and now this experience with the laced pot gave me negative feelings about using drugs. Looking back, I'm thinking it must have been laced with angel dust or something similar. When you get drugs from a stranger, you never know what you're getting.

Despite the argument over the laced drugs and the awkward incident with the Catholic priest, Candy and I still had a good last week together. If I had been an Australian or if she had been an American, we may have had a future together. However, we both knew that neither one of us was going to leave family, friends, and our home country to have a lasting relationship together.

Sue drove Candy and me to the train depot, so I could head back to Sydney. On the way to the depot, Candy and I sat in the back seat to talk and to give our sad farewells before my departure. Even though I had her address and phone number, I never saw or contacted Candy again. I didn't see the point in it. I assumed that she and Bob would eventually become an item together some day.

TWENTY-TWO DAYS AT SEA

Leaving a Dream Behind

I SPENT THE LAST COUPLE DAYS in Sydney at Antonio's. During the last few hours, I went through my personal belongings stored at his place for my trip home. Thoughts flooded my mind of so many of the wild, crazy events that I had experienced during my year in Australia. I decided to leave behind some of my things with Antonio, such as my motorcycle helmet, since I no longer had any use for it. I also left my road map, but I wish I had it now to help me remember more of the names of the places where I traveled.

Antonio drove me to the port of Sydney in time for me to board my ship. All my possessions were packed in the same footlocker that I came with, and more personal items were in my gym bag. While going through the process of boarding the ship, I had mixed emotions: I was excited for my first trip on an ocean liner, and eager to be returning home to America, but sad my Australian adventure had now come to an end.

Leaving Australia seemed a bit surreal until I felt the ship move away from the dock. Seeing an immense, seemingly never-ending span of ocean in front of me was proof that I was homeward bound.

The ship was a Greek ocean liner called *Australis*, with Chandris Lines. At the time, it was advertised as the "largest one class liner in the world," accommodating 2,000 passengers. Three weeks and a day is a long time to be on the water. Thankfully, the ship had an itinerary to help break up the long voyage with one-day stops along the way in New Zealand, the Fiji Islands, Acapulco, Balboa at the Panama Canal, and then finally to Miami.

TWENTY-TWO DAYS AT SEA

Rude and Crude

ON THE SHIP, the meals were served in a large dining room. Long rectangular tables covered with linen tablecloths seated eight to ten people each. No formal dress code was required. Greek waiters dressed in black pants, white shirts, and black vests served the passengers. Every day I sat at an assigned seat at the same table, with the same people, and the same waiter.

For some reason, our waiter chunked our plates of food down hard on the table in front of us. This rude gesture occurred with the very first meal on the first day.

One of the passengers eating at my table was a member of a heavy metal rock band. There were five members in the band on board, but for some reason, they were not all seated together. After a few days of continual mistreatment by our waiter, who always served us by flinging the plates of food down on the table, the heavy metal dude had had enough and took his plate of food and slammed it upside down on the table. Of course, he let out a few choice cuss words and demanded to see the waiter's supervisor. Needless to say, it was quite a scene.

The supervisor resolved the problem by moving the band member to a different table with a different waiter. I've always taken the approach that you don't want to piss off the people who serve your food. As you know, the servers or cooks could always spit in it—or worse.

* * *

Shortly after this incident, the same waiter approached me and gave me money to buy a bottle of whiskey for him because he said passengers could buy it cheaper than staff. Interestingly, after purchasing a bottle for him, I managed to get five-star service!

The rest of the band members didn't seem to be able to stay out of trouble either. One night, without permission, they decided to hook up their band equipment in the main ballroom and managed to blow out an amplifier. They were living up to the "ugly American" reputation of being rude and crude. And there was more bad behavior to come...

Night Moves...

MY SLEEPING QUARTERS were supposed to sleep four, but I managed to only have one other roommate and I hardly ever saw him. My first night, I was tired and with no one in my room to interrupt me, I should have slept like a baby; however, during the night I started having random sneezing attacks. I have allergies and I'm allergic to wool, and folded up on the ends of each of the beds were wool blankets to use if needed. I could have simply removed the blankets from my room, but the dank, musty smell could not be removed.

Exhausted and desperate for a good night's rest, I wondered if I could manage sleeping on deck by the pool. The ship's pool was filled with salt water from the ocean and was warm as bath water. I knew there usually weren't many people there in the daytime since most people, like me, in the heat of the day preferred to go for a cool and refreshing swim. When I approached the pool that night, I found it dimly lit and deserted. I got situated in a lounge chair, covered up with my beach towel, and, breathing the fresh salt air, I finally dozed off into a deep sleep.

* * *

This pleasant slumber was abruptly interrupted by a loud clap of thunder and before I could take cover, the bottom fell out. Now soaking wet, I was forced to gather up my drenched beach towel and head back to my cabin below deck to endure the rest of the night.

During that first week, I occasionally attempted to sleep by the pool at night, weather permitting. My sneezing attacks ceased, but sleeping on the deck continued to be a challenge since the weather the entire first week was cloudy and rainy. I finally met my porter on the ship and he removed the wool blankets and sprayed an aerosol disinfectant in my cabin. With the improved air quality, I could sleep in my cabin each night the rest of my time on board.

TWENTY-TWO DAYS AT SEA

New Zealand and the Fiji Islands

AT OUR FIRST STOP, New Zealand, we were allowed to disembark temporarily as our ship only docked there for one day. We weren't there long, but long enough to observe the native people with their tan complexions and dark hair. The Māori of New Zealand, I learned later, are indigenous Polynesian people, very much like the native Hawaiians, with their own language, crafts, performing arts, and customs. New Zealand turned out to be the prettiest place I've ever seen! It was mountainous, covered in all shades of green, with panoramic views of the ocean and huge rock cliffs. The views of New Zealand were a photographer's dream, but all I had was a Polaroid camera! I would love to go back sometime with a decent camera, more money, and more time.

Back on the ship again, I observed that the passengers consisted mainly of older married couples, some of whom were traveling around the world. The only younger, single, attractive lady whom I noticed on board just got off the ship back in New Zealand, our first stop after only one day's travel. Bummers!

I'm thinking, twenty-two days is a long time to be on a ship, especially with no girl prospects. Obviously, I was gonna have a lot of time to think about my life; a lot of time to think about what I was going to do when I got home. Temporarily, I would be staying with my grandmother, "Nannie," in Daytona Beach, but I knew I'd have to find another job after abruptly quitting the airlines, as well as another place to live. It was going to be a lonely trip home. Thankfully, I thought, the ship's itinerary should help to break up the monotony.

The Fiji Islands were our second stop. The Fiji Islands were known for having good prices on electronic equipment in addition to being duty-free.

Duty-free means that the stores or outlets were exempt from paying certain local or national taxes under the condition that the goods were sold to travelers who would take them out of the country. I had planned to buy a cassette stereo system with speakers that I could use in my house or the van that I planned to purchase when I got back to America. I did manage to get a great deal on a Kenwood stereo system with speakers.

Acapulco

OUR THIRD STOP, Acapulco, Mexico, was also beautiful, with its pristine beaches, swaying palm trees, and lush tropical vegetation. However, as soon as we got off the ship, we were bombarded by vendors and teenage kids trying to sell us anything and everything. In the eyes of the local people, all the passengers aboard the ship were assumed to be rich. Locals were trying to sell handmade items, hats, clothing; you name it, including drugs and prostitutes.

As you would imagine, knowing my fervent love for the ocean, I was one of several passengers who decided to take a little time to enjoy the beach. A couple ladies on our ship had gone swimming out in the water. The ocean water was a beautiful turquoise blue. I waded out into the smooth surf, which was so calm that it was more like a lake than an ocean. Suddenly, I heard the ladies holler out! I looked up just as a teenage boy scooped up their purses and belongings on the beach and took off running. I never found out exactly what happened, but I doubt they ever retrieved their belongings.

Paranoid that my wallet containing my ship pass and money left on the shore might be stolen next, I decided to get out of the water. I had hidden my wallet in my shirt, which sat on top of a beach towel. Relieved to retrieve my wallet, I put my shirt on over my wet swim trunks, put on my sandals, and decided to walk around in a vendor area not far from the beach.

* * *

Knowing I was out of pot, I thought, "What better place to buy Acapulco Gold marijuana than Acapulco?"

Not long after, a teenage boy approached me. In broken English he said, "I get you anything you want...girls, drugs..."

I responded, "I want to buy some good pot."

"I get you what you want," he said, "but you wait on me ten minutes."

When he returned, he had a folded newspaper with the pot hidden, rolled up inside. The teen was acting all paranoid as he handed me the newspaper. Instantly scanning my surroundings, I noticed two Federales, equivalent to "Feds" in the U.S., standing and talking nearby. Most everyone has heard of the nightmare stories of being locked up in a Mexican prison. Not wanting to go to prison, I quickly gave the boy twenty dollars and we went our separate ways.

I went to a more secluded part of the beach and opened the newspaper only to find it was full of seaweed. Lesson learned. Yes, Acapulco was beautiful, but warding off vendors and protecting yourself from locals constantly trying to rip you off, scam you, or lift your wallet right out of your pocket got old in a hurry. I should have known better, but I, like the two women on the beach, also got ripped off.

TWENTY-TWO DAYS AT SEA

How *Not* to Stop a Ship

EACH TIME PASSENGERS got off the ship at a port, we were reminded to return *on time*. Crew members made sure each passenger received a pamphlet with instructions about departing and re-boarding the ship. Emphasis was on the fact that the ship will not wait on you, and once the ocean liner sets sail, under no circumstances will it stop for you. It takes an enormous amount of fuel to get such a massive vessel stopped and started again.

After everyone boarded the ship in Acapulco, I stood on deck and watched as the ship slowly pulled out from the dock and began to pick up speed. As I felt the vibration beneath me and watched the wake increase behind us, I noticed a deep-sea fishing boat running wide open, approaching our moving ship. The boat was blowing its siren and the guys on board were frantically waving their arms as the boat came closer and began to run along the side of the ship. I angled for a better view of the fishing boat and saw five guys with long hair blowing in the wind. Well, remember the heavy metal rock and roll band? They were desperately trying to attract the captain's attention to stop the ocean liner. The captain must have noticed because the ship did slowly manage to come to a stop. Ship crew members lowered a rope ladder down to the "bad boys" of rock and roll. After the members of the band were finally on deck, they were ordered to the captain's quarters. I had fun watching the entire fiasco take place.

Later, I learned that the band had decided to go to a Mexican whorehouse and, obviously, took longer than they anticipated. I really don't know what happened in the captain's quarters that day, but I really would have liked to have been a fly on the wall to hear that conversation.

Tension in Panama

THE SHIP'S FOURTH STOP was at the port of Balboa, a town in Panama, just prior to passing through the Panama Canal. At that time, tensions were running high because Omar Torrijos, the dictator of Panama, wanted to take control of the Canal Zone. The ship's crew handed us flyers as we disembarked warning us to stay in groups because crime was so high in the area.

Three of us guys who regularly ate at the same table had pre-arranged to stay together when we got off the ship. As the three of us walked around the town, it was a bit unnerving to see that each street corner was manned with a Panamanian soldier holding an automatic rifle. It was also disturbing to see the native men and pretty women passing by us on the sidewalk who appeared to have knife scars on their faces.

We spotted another guy from the ship walking alone and noticed him entering a bar. To make sure he didn't get into any trouble, we decided to follow him inside. Entering the dimly lit bar out of the bright sunlight was haunting as we were temporarily blinded by the stark darkness. We could hardly see where to walk. A body could be lying in the corner and no one would even see it. After our eyes adjusted to the shadowy room, my gaze focused on the bartender. The native middle-aged, heavy-set man had a deep ugly scar on his face and a look about him that convinced me that he could kill his own mother.

* * *

We looked around for the missing lone passenger and found him sitting by himself at a table. We joined him and almost immediately two women pulled up chairs and sat down beside us. These "businesswomen of the night" began rubbing on our legs and motioning for us to come with them. I'm not the brightest apple of the bunch, but I'm pretty sure if we had left with them, we would have been mugged, or possibly worse. Little did they know that if they planned to rip me off, I had already spent most of my money on stereo equipment in Fiji and spent one of my last twenty-dollar bills on "seaweed" in Acapulco. Eventually, the girls took the hint that we weren't going anywhere with them and they left our table. Our group left the bar together and returned to the ship. Enough adventure for one day...

Passing through the huge locks of the Panama Canal was an awesome process to watch as they lowered and raised the water levels. It was interesting that on the right side of the canal was civilization, and on the left, was thick jungle thriving with monkeys and parrots. The green, lush, tropical jungle looked like a scene from a Tarzan movie.

Time for Soul-Searching

THE SHIP'S NEXT STOP would be my final stop: *Miami, Florida, USA!* I thought to myself. *Getting close! ALMOST HOME TO AMERICA!*

Twenty-two days is a long time to be on a ship, and it gave me a lot of time to think. I did a lot of soul searching, wondering what plans I had for the rest of my life. I had gone halfway around the world to Australia looking for greener grasses only to find that mankind is virtually the same everywhere on the earth. In America, we took the rich land away from the American Indians and stuck them in the desert while killing off the buffalo in the process. In Australia, they took the good land away from the Aborigines and stuck them in the desert and were killing off the kangaroos to make dog food.

I had been looking for a change when I left the red dirt of Georgia and traveled almost 10,000 miles only to see the *same red dirt* in Australia. This realization was like a big punch in the stomach and, needless to say, took the wind out of my sails. My disillusionment in my search for a better world and a new way of living, along with my quest for adventure and a desire to find peace in my life, left me with more turmoil than ever—and left me with a big hole in my heart.

BACK IN AMERICA

Going Through Customs

My ANXIETY WAS BUILDING as I thought of having to go through customs when I arrived back in the United States. If you remember, when I left America for Australia, the photo on my passport showed me clean cut with a short haircut. Now, after over a year, I was returning with a mustache, beard, and shoulder-length hair.

When we arrived in Miami, I waited in line to have my bags checked by the customs agent. When I handed him my passport, he looked down at my photo and back up at me three different times. The first words out of his mouth were, "I bet you smoked marijuana over there, didn't you, boy?" Laughing to myself, I assumed he was just feeling me out to see what kind of reaction he would get. I just played along with his game and lied, "No sir. I have enough problems without that." Really, I knew that I had nothing to worry about because if they searched me, I was clean. Looking like a hippie, I sure knew better than to carry any kind of contraband through customs!

After my bags were cleared, I left the customs station and stepped outdoors with my luggage. Looking around the area for my brother, Mike, who I had arranged to pick me up, I couldn't help but notice that compared to the Outback of Australia, Miami looked like a tropical paradise, with its tall graceful palm trees and fantastically lush, beautiful landscaping. I was so happy to once again have my feet on American soil that I literally got down on my knees and kissed the ground! I was so thankful to be back home!

BACK IN AMERICA

Seek and Find

WAITING IN THE SHADE of the passenger's pavilion pick-up area, I sat down on my footlocker to wait for Mike. Little did I know I would be waiting for two long hours! In all my excitement, it was a bit anticlimactic to return after such a long trip and have no one there to welcome me. The longer I had to wait, the more aggravated I got, knowing Mike had over a month to plan to be there on time. When he finally arrived, Mike said, "Sorry, I'm late, I misjudged how long it would take to drive from Daytona to Miami." I bit my lip as he helped me load my things into his car.

* * *

During the four-hour ride home to Daytona Beach, Mike and I had plenty of time to catch up on everything that had happened over the past 13 months. As I mentioned, during my last three weeks in Tasmania, I had received a letter from Mike saying that he found God and that he would explain in person. Mike began to share with me how painful it was going through his divorce. He told me how on a flight from Daytona to Atlanta, he was seated beside a Catholic priest named Father Tom. Mike believed it was "by the providence of God" that he happened to be seated by a priest during this turbulent time of his life. During his flight, Father Tom counseled my brother about his divorce and gave him his phone number in case he wanted further counseling.

When Mike returned to Atlanta, he met with Father Tom multiple times, not only for divorce counseling but also about his relationship with God. Mike had no desire to ever become a Catholic, nor was Father Tom pushing Catholicism. Father Tom was simply trying to point Mike toward God and Jesus Christ. It was obvious to me that Mike was seriously thinking about his spiritual relationship with God. He was setting up regular meetings, driving 80 miles round trip to Newnan to meet with Father Tom, about a one-hour drive each way from his place in Atlanta. Mike knew I was dealing with my own issues, so he invited me to attend one of his sessions with Father Tom. Since I, too, had so many questions about God and life in general, I agreed to tag along.

Like a lot of people, whether saved or unsaved, I had questions such as, "Why does God allow suffering of the innocent, especially children? Does God send people to hell? How do I find my purpose in life?" Father Tom recommended reading the four Gospels, which he said were four different accounts that were centered on the life of Christ. He explained to me that Jesus had set a perfect example for how each of us should live our lives. After several sessions, I still had many questions and was not ready to make any commitments.

* * *

During that time, my brother and I were staying with our mom in a huge apartment complex in the Atlanta area. Not long after I moved there, I met Rachel, a girl who lived in the same complex. Rachel was gorgeous with brown, wavy hair; in fact, she had just won a beauty pageant in Atlanta. She had been dating Ron, a lifeguard in the complex. To my advantage, they had recently broken up, and Rachel started dating me, probably on the rebound.

One day, Rachel called and said she would be right over. I thought it would be funny to play a trick on Rachel when she arrived. The front of each apartment had a mail slot in the lower part of the door for the postman to drop mail through. I thought about how long it should take her to walk over to my place. Shortly, I heard a knock on the door. I shoved my arm through the mail slot, grabbed her thigh, and goosed her up and down her leg REAL GOOD!

Immediately, with a big smile on my face, I opened the door only to see a young Boy Scout awkwardly backing up. With a terrified expression on his face, he held up a clipboard in his hand as he said, "Sir, I just wanted to know if you wanted to buy a raffle ticket?" Overwhelmed with sheer embarrassment, I volunteered to buy a couple raffle tickets that I would not have bought otherwise. Trying to act like nothing out of the ordinary happened, I did not acknowledge to the boy my bad behavior in any way.

Soon, I heard another knock on my door. Yes, this time, it *was* Rachel, and no, I had no desire to repeat my mail-slot trick.

BACK IN AMERICA

Cheap Shots

MIKE HAD BEFRIENDED RON the lifeguard, who had also recently been through a divorce. Ron and a buddy of his started coming over to our apartment to join me and Mike in Bible study twice a week. I was open to read and learn more about God and began devouring the words of the Bible on my own.

I had read through the Gospels as Father Tom had recommended, and I was working my way through the New Testament books in order. I read through the book of Acts, dealing with the history of the early church and the first Christians, and continued to read the rest of the New Testament, but the Book of James quickly became my favorite book. James seemed to be able to say in a sentence what others would say in a paragraph. This short book of only five chapters covers many topics, such as trials, persevering, the sin of partiality, faith and works, and things to avoid. I liked the book because what it has to say is so practical and tells you how to live your life. For example, James points out that no one can tame the tongue. The same tongue that praises God, curses God. James explains how a small spark can become a raging fire. I found that there was so much truth in the Book of James, like when it says that once you hurt someone with your words, you can't take it back. How real is that?

* * *

In my search for truth, I figured, if Christ is real, then so is Satan. In fact, now that we were seeking Christ in our lives, Satan was continually trying to trip us up—any way he could. For example, the following traps were set for both Ron and later for me.

Ron told us about a recent encounter with the *dark side*. He said, "A friend of mine offered to give me two pounds of marijuana that I could break down into one-ounce bags and make a small fortune…I did the right thing and turned it down, but I *sure* could have used the money." He added, "When I was into drugs, I probably would have never had such a tempting offer for free drugs to resell."

In *my* case, when I was back in Daytona Beach for a visit, I drove to a football stadium to see Santana and Buddy Miles live in concert. I was driving my hippie van that I had custom-painted a bright yellow and orange. Nannie had made curtains with matching yellow and orange dots for the windows. I was still proud to have my hippie-like appearance, with my long curly hair and headband.

As I was trying to find a place to park, a car with two pretty girls pulled up beside me and the girl driver motioned for me to roll down my window. She asked me if I wanted to park my van and go smoke a joint with them in their car. Not wanting to be a total square, I answered, "No, thanks. I'm trying to clean up my act." Both girls looked disappointed and, giving me a frown, proceeded to park their car a short distance away. I parked my van and noticed the girls getting out of their car and walking toward the concert. When I saw how fine they looked in their short shorts, I *whimpered* like a puppy dog. I was working on changing my behavior, but I *was* still a guy.

I call these attempts by Satan "cheap shots" because it was so obvious where the temptations were coming from. Meanwhile, I continued to study the Bible, and the more I read and learned, the more I knew what a sinner I was! I thought that by seeking God I would be happy, but I was becoming more miserable than ever! During the long time when I didn't know God and I had sinned, I didn't carry guilt. But now that I had read the words of God in the Bible, I was carrying a tremendous weight on my shoulders.

Moment of Truth

FATHER TOM HAD ATTEMPTED to answer some of my questions and my own search through the scriptures had answered many more, but I still had unanswered questions. From my study and seeking to know the truth, I finally came to the realization that the bottom line was my willingness to have faith for what I did not understand and have the willingness to change my life.

For years, my mom and Nannie had been on their knees, *literally*, praying for me daily. I discovered that *when you have prayer warriors praying for you, you can run, but there is nowhere to hide!* While alone one day in my mom's kitchen, the burden of sin became so overwhelming that I started crying. I reflected about my drug and alcohol abuse and about my selfish use of girls. I thought back about the scary experience I had with tripping grass at Candy's house; about my "scientific experiment" with opium in Tasmania and the dangerous situation I had put myself in with the drunken motorcycle gang. My mind even went to when I woke up on the bathroom floor from a hangover in Ft. Lauderdale after Luke and I got wasted at The Parrot nightclub. The painful and shameful thoughts flooded my mind and I pleaded to God for the forgiveness of my sins and asked Christ into my life.

Immediately, a great burden was lifted from my shoulders! A sense of joy and peace came over me and I felt like shouting from the rooftops about my salvation! That was just the start, however. My conversion was a lengthy process. It took almost two years for me to make a commitment from the day I began my search for God. But, really, it took the accumulation of all the years of Mama and Nannie's prayers for me, along with my journey and freedom to make bad choices to lead me to my salvation. No doubt, when Mama and Nannie learned that their prayers had finally been answered, they were shouting from the rooftops, too.

I knew it wasn't enough to say, "I believe," without making a real change in my life, so I immediately began to change up my act. I quit alcohol and marijuana cold turkey, and I also distanced myself from old friends who I knew might tempt me down the wrong path. I began spending more time with my newfound Christian friends.

As I said earlier, I was reading my Bible daily and searching the scriptures for answers. I read in the Gospel that when John the Baptist was baptizing people by the thousands, he also baptized Jesus Christ, the Son of God. I knew that water baptism by immersion was for the remission of sins and Jesus had no sin. I spent a while thinking about why Jesus, who was perfect, needed to be baptized. Finally, I decided that if it was important enough for Jesus to be baptized, then I should be baptized, too.

I didn't have a church home, but I felt led by the Holy Spirit to do this. I drove north of Atlanta to the Chattahoochee River and looked for a quiet, secluded place on the edge of the water. I parked the van and walked down into the river. When I got about waist-deep, I uttered the words, "Father, forgive me for my sins! Baptize me in the name of the Father, and the Son, and the Holy Ghost. Amen." I laid backwards into the water and submerged myself. As I stood back up and the water rolled off my head and face, knowing I had completed my act of obedience like Christ, I felt a sense of joy and peace. Act 2:38 says, *"Repent and be baptized, every one of you, in the name of Jesus Christ for the forgiveness of your sins. And you will receive the gift of the Holy Spirit."*

From my study of the Bible, I learned that the reason Jesus was baptized was to fulfill prophecy as well as to set an example for us. Over a year later, when I got comfortable enough to join a traditional church, I decided to be re-baptized by a minister publicly, hoping to be an encouragement to non-believers; however, I believe that God honored my "self-baptism," because I know it was led by the Holy Spirit.

Keeping It Real

IN 1972, AN AUSTRALIAN rock band called Daddy Cool released an album entitled "Sex, Dope, Rock 'n' Roll: Teenage Heaven." What a lost generation! And I had been a part of it… But God was at work, not only saving me, but saving members out of rock bands. Many, like me, had enough of the lie; namely, glorification of drugs and free sex as the answer to today's problems.

This was the time period when contemporary Christian music began to flourish. The pioneers of Christian-rock music included Larry Norman, called the "father of Christian rock," Phil Keaggy, considered one of the best Christian guitar players ever who sang solo, an amazing band called 2nd Chapter of Acts made up of two talented sisters and a brother, and the renowned Andréa Crouch, referred to as "the father of modern gospel music." The beginning of Christian rock music couldn't have happened at a better time, because even though I was saved, I still loved rock and roll. As Larry Norman said in his song, "Why should the devil have all the good music?"

All the girls liked Larry Norman, due to his good looks and long platinum blonde hair. I was a fan too. I heard he was going to sing one Friday night at a church in Atlanta, but when I got there, the concert had been cancelled. Rumor had it that the leadership got cold feet because of his hippie appearance and his rock-style Christian music. I suppose a church like this might have turned away Jesus Christ with His long hair, beard, mustache, and sandals. Well, I still got to see Larry Norman live in a small venue that night. The ironic part was that it wasn't at a church, it was in a bar. The owner had recently been saved and opened his business for the concert. No alcohol was served, of course. Yes, God was at work. He made sure the concert went on even if the church had dropped the ball.

At that time, the newly converted, hippie-like Christians were called "Jesus Freaks," and I was glad to be one. The established Christian churches didn't know how to deal with us because we didn't fit their cookie-cutter image of what a Christian should look like. A movement was started called "underground" churches. Groups commonly met in church basements at night and the services were usually led by youth ministers who were more open-minded toward hippie-type Christians.

I bounced around from one church to another trying to fit in yet feeling like most members of the established church were hypocrites. I felt like if church members were really Christ-like, they would be more accepting of me and others who looked like hippies. This troubled me, so I arranged a meeting with a minister of one of these churches. I complained to the minister, "The church is full of hypocrites."

He responded, "Pat, you can shop around for the perfect church, but as soon as you join it, it's not perfect anymore."

"Ouch!" I thought. "The truth hurts."

From my study of the Bible, I was fully aware of the scripture in Romans 3:23, *"For all have sinned and come short of the glory of God."* Through the years, as I matured as a Christian, I have learned that the church is made up of "sinners." Yes, some are hypocrites, but the difference is that *true* Christians have repented of their sins, try not to repeat their sins, and ask for the grace of God in their lives.

From personal experience, I have also learned that becoming a Christian does not mean life will be a bed of roses, as bad things still happen. I ended up going through both a divorce and a bankruptcy, both ugly, life-changing events. The difference is, being a Christian, I didn't have to go through these painful events alone. With God and the help of my Christian friends, I not only had the hope of merely surviving, but actually, I fully recovered and have even flourished in my life once again.

EPILOGUE

LITTLE DID I KNOW my wild-haired plan to escape for an Australian adventure would affect the rest of my life! I did everything I thought would make me satisfied and happy. I tried and experimented, with no moral compass, in pursuit of fulfillment. But the pleasure I found was merely temporary and left me with a hole in my heart.

* * *

Amazingly, God had a plan. By allowing me the freedom to explore and follow my own path, He opened my eyes to His will for my life. I suppose I had to "experience life" to know that my plan wasn't as perfect as I had originally thought. I had a good job, a cool car, money in the bank, and lived only 10 minutes from the beach, yet I was willing to give it all up to seek happiness elsewhere. It took the emptiness in my life for God to teach me that true happiness could not be found in either material goods or my quest for greener grasses.

Hopefully, my experiences that you have read in this book will save you from a "ten-thousand-mile trip" only to find the SAME RED DIRT. Peace only comes from God and from within. I pray that if you have a hole in your heart, that you will come to know the Prince of Peace, Jesus Christ.

Before You Go...

If you enjoyed my book, SAME RED DIRT, please post a review on your favorite bookstore's website or social media pages.

Thank you for reading!

--Pat Conrad

ABOUT THE AUTHOR

BORN AND RAISED in Daytona Beach, Florida, Pat Conrad graduated from Seabreeze High School in 1967 and a year later, moved to the red dirt hills of Georgia. Although his intense love for the beach will never die, Pat and his family have all adopted north Georgia as their home, where Pat is an avid outdoorsman. Pat lives with his wife Vicki and has two grown children, Zack and Charity, and five beautiful grandchildren. Currently, he and Vicki enjoy living in the country outside of Toccoa, Georgia. They are both active at Toccoa Christian Church, where Pat serves as an elder.